Modern
Parliamentary
Procedure

Modern Parliamentary Procedure

Ray E. Keesey

University of Delaware

Houghton Mifflin Company
Boston

Atlanta
Dallas
Geneva, Illinois
Hopewell, New Jersey
Palo Alto
London

Printed in the U.S.A.

Library of Congress Catalog Card Number: 73–8073

ISBN: 0–395–17015–X

To two friends,
whose encouragement prompted me to undertake
the simplification of parliamentary rules
for the conduct of meetings:
G. Bruce Dearing and John W. Shirley

Contents

Foreword

Robert W. English

Founder, American Institute of Parliamentarians

Dr. Keesey's book, *Modern Parliamentary Procedure*, is a giant step toward the much needed
modernization of parliamentary procedure and
toward the better implementation of the fundamental principle that parliamentary procedure
should facilitate the transaction of business in an
orderly, deliberative, democratic manner.

For decades there has been a serious need for
a modern book on parliamentary procedure, one
that would serve as a suitable, up-to-date parliamentary authority, textbook, and reference
book, a book acceptable to the vast number who
dislike the misleading terminology and ill-advised
complications of parliamentary orthodoxy. Dr.
Keesey's book fulfills this need and improves parliamentary procedure so that it is easier for vital,
controversial issues to be solved by parliamentary
means rather than by violence or dictatorial
action.

Modern Parliamentary Procedure presents numer-
ous methods for more efficient democratic action.
Its contributions include modernizing parliamentary terminology, presenting a simpler and more
logical classification of motions, eliminating
several troublesome, superfluous motions, and
providing some valuable ideas concerning the
prevention and handling of disruptions. There is
also a liberal amount of teaching material, which
makes this a valuable textbook as well as a parliamentary authority.

Foreword

Robert C. Jeffrey

Chairman, Department of Speech Communication
The University of Texas at Austin

Both teachers and students will appreciate *Modern Parliamentary Procedure* because it not only provides a clear understanding of parliamentary principles and their application, but it makes operative again their democratic purpose.

Deliberative assemblies can be democratic only to the extent that the individual members are free to participate in all of the proceedings, not just voting. Individual freedom is effectively limited when the rules of an organization are so complicated and technical that members are intimidated by the awesomeness of the rule book. This can lead to autocratic rule by a professionally trained chairman or by part of the membership. For this reason the procedural and substantive rights of members of deliberative and legislative bodies are equally important to voting. Consequently, anything that can be done to simplify the rules to permit all to play the game with equality is a victory for the democratic process.

Ray Keesey's *Modern Parliamentary Procedure* makes this equality possible. It satisfies a growing need to simplify rules of order governing all but the most legalistic and formal groups. But this book is more than a simplification of existing rules; it is a new procedural design. Keesey has reduced the number of useful motions to a manageable thirteen and divides the motions into two groups instead of four. The student of this book will not feel intimidated; its contents can be memorized and can be useful for all after a relatively short period of study and practice.

The plan of *Modern Parliamentary Procedure* for conducting business within groups is revolutionary to the extent that the motions (and the rules for their use) are unfettered with exceptions and legalistic jargon. It is the most usable book on parliamentary procedure to be devised since the simplest forms constructed centuries ago in England and it represents a significant contribution to democratic participation in decision-making assemblies. The teacher of parliamentary procedure could not ask for a better text.

Preface

This is a textbook and manual of simplified parliamentary procedure, entirely compatible with accepted parliamentary principles but free of the traditional mysterious jargon of the professional parliamentarian. This book's specific points of departure from other manuals of parliamentary procedure are:

1. Reduction in the number of motions
2. Simplified precedence of motions
3. Elimination of the "seconding" of motions
4. Emphasis on the principle of majority rule.

The procedure is truly simplified. The total number of motions is considerably reduced, and each motion says exactly what it means, requiring no restatement or translation by the presiding officer. Superfluous motions have been eliminated, and "subsidiary and privileged motions" have been combined into the single category, Ordinary Motions. Unnecessary and confusing motions have been relegated to Chapter 6, "Motions Not Recommended." Many distinctions in the rank of precedence of motions have been eliminated, and the student or group member will find less rote memory required for effective participation in meetings. Time will be saved by not insisting on the seconding of motions. In general, stressing a more straightforward and open procedure for meetings eliminates the parliamentary impasses that appear to follow when too much attention is given to parliamentary intrigue and manipulation. It is therefore easier to participate in a meeting conducted under the rules in *Modern Parliamentary Procedure*, and the authority for flexibility in administering rules rests firmly in the assembly itself. In this way organizations using *Modern Parliamentary Procedure* will find their meetings more democratic in operation.

As a textbook *Modern Parliamentary Procedure* is designed to be helpful to both teacher and student. There are at the back of the book more than enough exercises to assure the practical application and understanding of each chapter. In addition, there is space in the margins to take all the notes important for study or special reference, the kind of personal record that makes a book worth keeping.

R. E. K.

Modern
Parliamentary
Procedure

Introduction

Introduction

Winston Churchill is said to have remarked that legislative procedure is an enigma wrapped in a mystery. It should not be mysterious. For one thing, most people do not need to know all of its rules. In selecting rules for inclusion here, I have made a fresh beginning, taking nothing as sacrosanct. My operating principle has been to ask, "What really is essential?" to a group considering a proposition. The result, I believe, makes the democratic principles of parliamentary procedure much more functional.

Progress in simplifying parliamentary rules has already been made by Hellman, by Sturgis, and by other recognized authorities.[1] Further simplification of the procedural rules is needed particularly by groups that operate without benefit of a parliamentarian.

I originally hoped to advocate fewer rules, perhaps in entirely new terminology. However, practical considerations, growing out of more than twenty years' experience as a parliamentarian and a continuing interest in the subject as student and teacher, argue against further simplification. Fairness in the handling of motions, the

[1]Hugo Hellman, *Parliamentary Procedure* (New York: Macmillan, 1966); Alice Sturgis, *Sturgis Standard Code of Parliamentary Procedure*, 2nd ed. (New York: McGraw-Hill, 1966). See also Robert M. English, "A New View of Subsidiary Motions," *Parliamentary Journal* 10 (January, 1969); 19–23.

flexibility to modify motions before voting, and freedom to rectify mistakes after a vote has been taken must be assured by rules known to all.

A Basic Parliamentary Approach
Groups need to know the rules only for those motions they normally use; most other specially required procedures may be formulated, and their limitations agreed to, by majority vote *at the time the need arises*. As any experienced parliamentarian knows, special situations do arise that call for procedures not covered specifically in any manual. The exercise of common sense by the presiding officer and parliamentarian, consistent with the basic principles of parliamentary procedure discussed in Chapter 1, should point the way to solutions. The assembly's approval of any special procedures should be invited by the presiding officer whenever feasible. This is discussed more fully in Chapter 7.

Simplified Rules and Terminology
The rules of parliamentary procedure tell how, when, and why to use motions. A *motion* is a form of expression, usually beginning with the familiar and time-honored words "I move that . . .", used to present ideas to a group for consideration.

What rules are essential? *Robert's Rules of Order Newly Revised* lists more than eighty motions. Busy members of voluntary organizations cannot be expected to memorize these, as well as the six or eight categories that apply to each motion.

In a few cases, rules have been simplified by allowing one motion to serve purposes that previously required separate motions. In other instances, actions previously undertaken only by means of formal motions may now be accomplished without the use of motions at all. Those who question the wisdom of omitting some of the traditional motions will find in Chapter 6 a list of those no longer recommended, with a brief explanation for the exclusion of each.

A compelling reason for following acceptable procedure is the possibility of a court action brought by a person who feels that his interests have been slighted. Thousands of court cases in which the verdict turned on the validity of a decision-making procedure have been examined by Mason and Sturgis.[2] Mason defines *parliamentary law* as the rules and principles that the courts apply in judging a controversy growing out of the process of decision making.[3] The law presumes that deliberative groups will follow their own constitutions, bylaws, and rules, and in all cases not covered by these will be governed by parliamentary law.

Court decisions have been handed down protecting the right of a minority to be heard, defining a majority vote, outlining the authority of tellers in handling secret ballots, forbidding the secretary to cast a unanimous ballot in elections, defending the right to freedom of debate, among other issues. Members of an organization, as well as the presiding officer and parliamentarian, should understand the need to follow acceptable procedures. This is not meant to imply that any special procedures can assure that group decisions will be legal. As O'Brien points out, skill in the use of acceptable parliamentary procedure is more practicable than a broad knowledge of civil law and its relation to parliamentary procedure.[4]

Legal Requirements for Procedure

[2]Paul Mason, *Mason's Manual of Legislative Procedures*, (New York; McGraw-Hill, 1953); Sturgis, *Sturgis Standard Code*.

[3]Paul Mason, "The Law and Parliamentary Procedures" *Adult Leadership* 5 (December, 1956): 188–190. James W. Cleary, one of four collaborators on *Robert's Rules of Order Newly Revised*, takes the somewhat different position that rules of order are firmly based on the principles and practices of voluntary democratic organizations and do not depend for their validity on court decisions. See "A Commentary on Robert's Rules of Order Newly Revised" *Parliamentary Journal* 9 (April, 1968); 3–9. Since court decisions are largely based on precedent, it is advisable for any organization to avoid procedural practices that the courts have found invalid.

[4]J. F. O'Brien, *Parliamentary Law for the Layman* (New York: Harper and Bros., 1952), p. 208.

The Parliamentary Authority

A *parliamentary authority*, once adopted in an organization's bylaws, becomes the basic source of its procedural rules. A parliamentarian advising a presiding officer is expected to follow the adopted parliamentary authority, whether or not he would prefer another. Organizations that find *Modern Parliamentary Procedure* to their liking should amend their bylaws to adopt it as their parliamentary authority. Otherwise, the benefits of its innovations may not be available to them.

Designation of the Presiding Officer

The presiding officer has traditionally been called the chairman. The word "chairman" has been used for many years as a generic term applied to both sexes. Recently, however, the term chairperson has been chosen by many organizations as a more suitable generic designation. In practice the presiding officer of most groups is the president, who, when presiding, may still be called president. "Presiding officer," "president," "moderator," "the chair," "chairman," "chairwoman," and "chairperson" are all appropriate designations depending upon the circumstances and the usage assigned by an organization in its bylaws. It should be up to individual groups to select and vary the use of these terms as they see fit.

In this book the masculine pronoun when it refers to the presiding officer or to the member of an organization represents both woman and man, according to the linguistic convention of English.

Summary

A need exists for greater simplification of parliamentary procedure, despite previous efforts in this direction. Many organizations have adopted a parliamentary authority not generally understood by their members. A large portion of the most frequently adopted parliamentary authority is probably too complicated for most members of volunteer organizations, who cannot be expected to do the detailed study necessary to understand it. And much of it is unnecessary for such organizations.

The Basic Principles

1

The Basic Principles

As Jefferson put it, "The voice of the majority decides." This principle (*lex majoris partis*) is at the heart of democratic procedure. It is another way of saying that conflicts may be resolved by agreeing to accept a decision, solution, or recommendation approved by more than half of those voting. It assumes—and the principle is not workable otherwise—that those in the minority agree to accept the decision of the majority. Whether or not it is stated as a condition of membership, any member of an organization whose meetings are governed by parliamentary procedure agrees to abide by the mandate of the majority.

In a very real sense, the observation of parliamentary rules is the surest way to determine the opinion of the majority. Under no circumstances may a group suspend the *principle* of majority rule. It may adopt certain rules for its own use, such as a rule closing debate by a two-thirds vote, but in the absence of any special rule to the contrary, the majority of the eligible votes cast, assuming a quorum present, represents the will of the majority. By applying the principle of majority rule any group may decide what it is willing to consider and what it is not willing to consider. It may postpone consideration until a more convenient time, or it may modify any pending proposal to make it represent the will of the majority. Finally, it may decide at any time to adjourn the meeting.

Description and Discussion
Majority Rule

Although a quorum must be present for an organization to conduct business legally (except in those few circumstances listed on page 33), a quorum is usually no more than half the membership, and sometimes considerably less. Therefore, a legal majority may in fact be a majority of a minority, and the actual votes cast for the majority decision may represent a small fraction of the group's total membership, or even of a quorum.

The Rights of
the Minority

During the decision-making process, the apparent minority has the right to be heard, to oppose what appears to be the majority's position, and to try to persuade others to accept its point of view. It is often not known until the vote is taken which position has the majority. A member voting with the minority retains all the rights and privileges of membership, and may not be discriminated against because of his vote. He may not be forced to vote on any question. He has the same right as any other member to propose a motion, and to speak and vote for or against a motion.

While accepting the majority's decision, the minority member may continue to plan strategy intended eventually to make the minority's point of view that of the majority. For example, when a committee reports to its parent group, a minority report may be presented as an amendment to the committee report, and a vote taken on substituting the minority report for the committee report. This subject is discussed further under Committee Reports in Chapter 8.

Many parliamentary rules are intended specifically to protect the rights of members of the minority. He may not be deprived of his right to debate unless a vote to that effect (usually requiring two-thirds) passes; he may expect that the agenda will be covered in the order specified in the call for the meeting (unless two-thirds vote to suspend the rules); he may not be deprived of the right to have his proposal considered (unless a majority votes to remove his motion from consideration); and he may assume that certain actions, such as amending a bylaw, will not be taken in a meeting unless he has received previous notice, as specified in the bylaws, that they are to be considered.

Each member of a deliberative organization conducting its affairs in accordance with parliamentary procedure has the same rights, privileges, and duties as any other member. He has the right to present his proposition for consideration, to discuss and recommend it for adoption, and to have it critically examined by his colleagues before a vote is taken. He has a right to demand that the presiding officer put propositions above personalities and call on members as they request the floor, trying to balance the expression of pro and con arguments on a proposition, and not permitting a one-sided presentation.

Equality of Members

He has the right to be nominated for office and to have his election to office determined by secret ballot. He has a right to expect courteous treatment from others when he has the floor, and a duty to extend this courtesy to others. He has a right to expect that the parliamentary rules of an organization will be fairly administered, and he may not be denied the privileges of attending meetings and participating on an equal basis with all of the members. He may expect that his vote will carry the same weight as that of any other member, and that he may, if he wishes, refrain from voting.

The right to be heard and to hear what others have to say about a motion before voting on it is basic to intelligent group action. How one votes may well be determined by evidence, analysis, and persuasion presented during the discussion of a motion. Freedom of discussion is integral to other basic principles, including the rule of the majority, the rights of the minority, and equality of membership. No member may have his right

Freedom of Discussion

to "speak his piece" circumscribed, except by rules that similarly limit the rights of all of the members. The motion to close debate is misused if it is offered to prevent members from stating their views. Since such a motion deprives a minority of freedom of debate, it requires a two-thirds vote to pass. Its use should be infrequent, and is only justified to prevent repetition of argument when it is apparent that little is to be gained from further discussion. It may be used to deter a small but vocal minority from pressing its position to the point of exhausting and exasperating an apparent majority.

Other Principles The rule of the majority, the rights of the minority, equality of membership, and freedom of discussion are the four most fundamental principles of democratic action. Parliamentary rules of procedure exist to insure their observance. Mention should be made of some other principles, perhaps less crucial but important for a more complete understanding of the need for certain parliamentary rules. Among them are:

1. Only one main motion may be considered at any given time.
2. Members have a right to know at all times what the immediately pending motion is, and to have it restated before a vote is taken.
3. Organizations may take official action only in meetings properly called, and with a quorum of members present.
4. Actions taken by organizations are not valid if they tend to subvert either the civil laws of the nation, state, or local governmental unit or the rules of a parent organization.

The principles of parliamentary law may appear self-evident, or indistinguishable from those on which all democracies are based—as indeed they are. But it cannot be too heavily emphasized that blind adherence to parliamentary rules without an appreciation of their relation to democratic principles can only lead to a shallow conception of their real purpose. On the other hand, proper appreciation of these principles may result in an attitude toward administration of the rules that will guide a presiding officer or a member to wise and tolerant participation in group meetings.[1]

When a group is capable of decision making in an informal way, without the use of parliamentary rules, it should do so. This type of meeting usually requires a group small enough to permit considerable informality, and a patience and sophistication in human relations rarely shared by all the members. It is wrong, however, to insist that all groups, regardless of size and also degree of internal harmony, hold to the letter of all parliamentary rules. O'Brien recommends that the degree of procedural formality be adapted to the group's unity, size, and knowledge of acceptable parliamentary procedure.[2]

Some Groups Require More Rules Than Others

In small groups, certainly including committee meetings, informal procedures are often preferable. The presiding officer should request a formal vote only when a decision must be made and unanimity seems impossible within the time available. In small informal groups it may be helpful to discuss the wording of a motion before actually proposing it, thereby avoiding the time-consuming process of amending the motion to reach the agreed form. In all such proceedings the presiding officer may save time by using the informal procedure of general consent. That is, when group opinion appears to have crystallized, the presiding officer may announce, "If there is no objection, we will. . . ." Members, of course, must be ready to prevent abuse of this procedure; a single objection forces a vote.

Recent research in social psychology, problems of group development, and the dynamics of decision making, have led some to feel that voting is less

Arguments for Limiting the Use of Parliamentary Procedure

[1]Giles W. Gray, "A Philosophy of Parliamentary Law," *Quarterly Journal of Speech* 27 (October, 1941): 437–441.

[2]J. F. O'Brien, *Parliamentary Law for the Layman* (New York: Harper and Bros., 1952), p. xvii.

desirable than consensus as a means to decide questions. The Quakers have long been highly respected for their practice of taking "the sense of the meeting."[3]

Some have argued against using parliamentary procedure in decision making. One of the most common criticisms is that its use invites polarization within a group, the forces for a motion aligning against those opposed to it. Many decisions are arrived at only by the narrowest of margins, in a climate of *winning* and *losing*—not the best atmosphere for the enthusiastic and cooperative implementation of decisions. It also tends to discourage individuals from feeling a personal responsibility for decisions or for their fulfillment.

Other arguments could be marshaled in favor of approaching a problem-solving or decision-making situation without resorting to parliamentary rules. Such groups probably do, however, use a crude form of parliamentary procedure, and, of course, effectiveness is not assured by abandoning acceptable parliamentary procedure. It is possible that this point of view may mask a failure to study the basic rules of procedure, and a resulting ignorance of the flexibility possible within good parliamentary practice.[4]

When Parliamentary Procedure Is Required

There are valid arguments for suspending parliamentary procedure under some circumstances. Cooperative problem-solving groups with enough time available will usually discover within their ranks leaders who can guide them to wise decisions. But many groups cannot operate in this way. Time is limited; problems are pressing; action is required. In these cases the needs of the group tend to make preferable a more formal method of proceeding, involving the observance

[3]See Morris Llewellyn Cooke, "The Quaker Way Wins New Adherents," *The New York Times Magazine* 6 (June 17, 1951): 21, 40–42. Reprinted in *Parliamentary Journal* 5 (October, 1965): 12–18.

[4]See Irving J. Lee, *How to Talk With People* (New York: Harper and Bros., 1952), for an enlightening discussion of difficulties commonly encountered when groups "talk together."

of common-sense rules to insure that all members have an equal opportunity to participate, that minorities are not ignored, that the rule of the majority prevails, and the like. When groups cannot unite on the issues before them, and especially when time is a factor—as it always is, parliamentary procedure appears to be the best solution.[5]

Fortunately, when groups turn to more formal procedures they need not improvise rules. The path is well marked. They have at their disposal basic principles that have stood the test of time. The rules of procedure may vary according to the type of group, and may be suspended to meet a specific need or changed, if the group desires. But the principles do not vary, and may be neither suspended nor changed. The rules of parliamentary procedure exist to protect the observance of democratic principles. Differences of opinion on procedural matters may often be resolved by asking how to insure that basic principles are not violated.

[5]For an interesting development of this point by a leader of the "group dynamics" approach, see Franklyn S. Haiman, *Group Leadership and Democratic Action* (New York: Houghton Mifflin, 1951) Chapter 10.

A Historical Sketch
of Parliamentary Procedure

2

A Historical Sketch
of Parliamentary Procedure

The basic principles of parliamentary procedure appear to have been clearly defined and practiced as early as the fifth century B.C. in Athens.[1] The Bible describes the Council of Seventy chosen to assist Moses, and there are references to deliberative assemblies in the Hebrew commonwealth as far back as 1200 B.C.

The assembly (*ecclesia*) of Athens met regularly, usually on a hill called the Pynx, to listen to their spokesmen speak from a rock platform called the *bema*. The speakers were often military leaders reporting on their campaigns, or political leaders such as Pericles or Demosthenes. The assembly had prepared agenda, was presided over by a chairman, listened to all those who wished to speak, passed motions to prevent or limit debate as needed, and voted—usually by a show of hands—on propositions before them.

The highest deliberative authority in the Roman republic was the Senate. Composed of magistrates, not popular representatives, this group observed great formality in dress, tradition, and

---

[1] J. F. O'Brien, "Historical Development of Parliamentary Discussion," *The Thomas Jefferson Parliamentarian* 4 (November, 1960): 3–19, and 4 (May, 1961) 1–20. Reprinted in *Parliamentary Journal* in three parts in October, 1966; January, 1967; and April, 1967. O'Brien's article, to which this chapter is indebted, should be read by those interested in further information.

procedure. Other assemblies of lesser rank existed, but the Roman Senate, because of distinguished leadership exercised by the most outstanding men of the time, became universally respected for its soundness of judgment and wise counsel. In its deliberations, clarity and brevity were applauded, and the "purple patches" of oratorical greatness of Cicero probably represented an exception to the general atmosphere.

The English Tradition

When the colonial congress of the United States was looking for procedure to govern its deliberations, it naturally turned to that used by the British Parliament. Parliamentary procedure in England had evolved through precedent from as early as the thirteenth century, and was fairly well developed by the eighteenth century. A compilation of these rulings was published by John Hatsell, clerk of the House of Commons, in two volumes, one in 1776 and the second in 1781, and later reissued in four volumes. Referred to as *Hatsell's Precedents*, these volumes were the principal source of Thomas Jefferson's *Manual of Parliamentary Practice*, published in 1801. A written record of the proceedings of Parliament, often of doubtful authenticity, has been kept from 1509 for the House of Lords and from 1547 for the House of Commons. Not until 1908 did both Houses instigate an official recording of proceedings, no longer relying on private records.

Parliamentary Procedure in the United States

The development of parliamentary procedure in the United States after the adoption of the procedure followed in the British Parliament, is best illustrated by a brief look at the three principal writers on the subject prior to the twentieth century: Jefferson, Cushing, and Robert.

Thomas Jefferson, as vice president and presiding officer of the United States Senate, recognized the need for a compilation of the rules of procedure, adapted largely from *Hatsell's Precedents*, he thought appropriate for Senate use. His *Manual of Parliamentary Practice*, published in 1801, the first year of his presidency, continues to be the principal parliamentary guide of the Senate and the House of Representatives, the latter having adopted it in 1837. Jefferson's *Manual* was the first significant publication on parliamentary procedure in the United States.

The extent of its influence was probably not anticipated by Jefferson, who wrote modestly of his own role as that of a "mere compiler" and did not consider the *Manual* worthy of inclusion in a proposed complete edition of his writings. His own original contribution he limited to the arrangement of the material, and "a few observations" and examples.[2]

The second most significant publication on parliamentary procedure was by a Massachusetts lawyer and judge, Luther Stearns Cushing. Drawing on his experience as clerk of the Massachusetts House of Representatives from 1832 to 1834, Cushing wrote *A Manual of Parliamentary Practice; Rules of Proceedings and Debate in Deliberative Assemblies*. Published in 1845, it was generally known as *Cushing's Manual*. Considered more appropriate to the needs of nonlegislative groups than Jefferson's *Manual*, it was also widely

Thomas Jefferson

Luther S. Cushing

[2]Letter to John W. Campbell dated September 3, 1809, in *The Writings of Thomas Jefferson*, edited by Paul Leicester Ford (New York: G. P. Putnam's Sons, 1898) 9: 258. For more information on Jefferson's *Manual*, all in the *Parliamentary Journal*, see Richard S. Kain, "America's Parliamentary Inheritance from Thomas Jefferson," 7 (April, 1966): 14–18; Thais M. Plaisted, "Noted Legal Writers Quoted by Jefferson," 9 (January, 1968): 13–18, and "Historical Footnotes in Jefferson's *Manual*" 10 (January, 1969): 3–13.

used by legislative groups. Only four inches by six inches in its best-known form, *Cushing's Manual* sold extensively in the United States and abroad.[3]

Henry M. Robert The most widely used book on parliamentary procedure today is that of Henry M. Robert. The seventy-fifth anniversary edition of *Robert's Rules of Order Revised* (1951) representing the third revised edition, was preceded by four editions of the original *Pocket Manual of Rules of Order* first published in 1876. A new edition, entitled *Robert's Rules of Order Newly Revised* (1970), has grown from 326 pages in the 1951 edition to 594 pages, mostly due to an increase in the number of illustrations and examples.

Robert was an army engineer and a successful promoter of his manual, which is characterized by a degree of detail and an emphasis on parliamentary strategy regarded by some as more extensive than necessary. Robert apparently invented some rules to meet needs as he saw them. Some of his highly technical distinctions and lengthy observations appear unnecessarily complicated for the procedural requirements of many volunteer organizations today. Robert made a signal contribution, however, in calling the attention of thousands to the need for the study and practice of parliamentary procedure. He also attempted to standardize and to stabilize the rules of procedure for nonlegislative groups. In this his efforts were so successful that for many of his followers his rules became almost synonomous with parliamentary law itself. *Robert's Rules of Order* is today, however, and was from the beginning, only one system adapted to this purpose.

[3]Cushing also published a longer, more legalistic work, Lex Parliamentaria, *Law and Practice of Legislative Assemblies*, in 1856.

None of the guides to parliamentary procedure since *Robert's Rules of Order* has had as wide an acceptance as his. Some of the better known ones are by Auer, Davidson, Demeter, Hellman, Mason, O'Brien, and Sturgis. Of these the one by Alice Sturgis is probably best known. A few writers (Demeter, Mason, Sturgis) have gone to some lengths to show how court decisions and legal precedents stand as a basis for parliamentary rules. Others (O'Brien, Davidson) appear to accept the position that the rules are firmly grounded in the accepted practices of voluntary organizations and do not depend upon the sanction of the courts for their validity. Robert is a member of this latter group.

In addition to individual writers, many organizations have published parliamentary guides for their members. These include such large organizations as the American Medical Association, the Federated Women's Clubs, and Toastmasters International. These groups follow the practice that Robert himself found useful; when necessary, they invent or adapt rules to meet their particular needs. Any such special rules take precedence over those found in the adopted parliamentary authority.

Introduction to the Rules of Procedure

3

Introduction to
the Rules of Procedure

The term *precedence* refers to the rank of a motion in an established, or agreed-to, order for motions. Knowing the precedence for a motion, a member knows when the motion may be made and when it would be *out of order*.

Precedence of Ordinary Motions
1. To Adjourn
2. To Recess
3. To Close Debate
4. To Limit (Extend the Limits of) Debate
5. To Postpone
6. To Refer
7. To Amend

The motion To Adjourn has the highest rank or precedence. This means that To Adjourn is in order even though other motions are pending. On the other hand, a motion of low precedence, or rank, may not be made if one of higher rank is under consideration. For example, a motion To Amend is out of order if offered when To Refer is pending; it would be in order only if nothing of higher rank than the main motion were under consideration. Similarly, To Recess is out of order while To Adjourn is pending, but To Recess would be in order if To Amend and To Postpone had both been moved and the latter (of higher rank than To Amend) was under consideration. A main motion has the lowest rank of all. Most of the seven ordinary motions exist to facilitate the efforts of an assembly to arrive at a decision on a main motion. Precedence or rank among motions prevents confusion. Memorizing the precedence of motions is less difficult when there are fewer kinds of motions involved.

Special Motions

Point of Order
To Appeal
To Withdraw
To Suspend the Rules
To Reconsider
To Rescind

Special motions have no rank in relation to each other. There is no necessary or predefined relationship among them. Except for To Reconsider and To Rescind, they exist largely to handle procedural matters that arise during the consideration of a main motion.

A Point of Order is in order at any time, depending on its urgency, and may be followed by To Appeal. To Withdraw may be used at any time except to disrupt voting or to interrupt a speaker. To Suspend the Rules may be offered if a motion is pending, as may To Reconsider. All but Point of Order and To Withdraw are handled like any other main motion if moved when no main motion is pending. To Rescind is not in order if another main motion is under consideration.

Thus, in addition to the main motion, there are seven ordinary motions and six special motions. Only three of the thirteen require a two-thirds vote: To Limit (Extend the Limit of) Debate, To Close Debate, and To Suspend the Rules; all others need only a majority vote to pass. Most meetings will use only a few of the ordinary motions. In many meetings no special motions at all are introduced.

Any organization should feel free to modify the order of precedence when it appears desirable, either by general consent or by suspending the rules with a two-thirds vote. Thus, if a member moves to postpone the consideration of a question with a proposed amendment until a later meeting, and it appears wiser to refer the consideration to a committee, there is no reason why, by general consent, the motion To Refer to a committee may not be considered, even if To Postpone has been moved and stated by the chair. If To Refer is passed, the motion To Postpone is, of course, ignored and the main motion and its proposed amendment are sent to a committee for its recommendation. The point is that rules exist to serve the group, not the reverse.

Among the special motions, only To Suspend the Rules requires a two-thirds vote. A Point of Order (which is a request or a demand, not a motion), To Withdraw, and To Suspend the Rules are not debatable, and only one of the six, To Rescind, may be amended.

Seconding of Motions

Motions need not be seconded. The requirement of a second is largely a waste of time. What member is so destitute of friends that he can't find one willing to second his motion? The traditional justification for requiring a second is that at least two members should support a motion to justify its consideration. In practice, presiding officers routinely drone "Do I hear a second?" after each motion proposed, regardless of its merit and obvious appropriateness, and many members volunteer a "second the motion" even before the presiding officer's request. Often members do not understand the relevance or desirability of a motion until pertinent information is revealed in discussion. There is nothing essentially *wrong* with the practice of seconding. It is simply unnecessary. It approaches the ridiculous when the chairperson of a committee whose members are facing each other around a table, requires that one member second another's motion. Time wasted on this ritual should be saved for more fruitful purposes.

If seconding is intended to prevent frivolous and unnecessary motions from being offered, it is an ineffective deterrent since there is no reason to assume that only one member is so inclined. Control of unnecessary motions is best exercised by the presiding officer who should address a few simple questions to the mover of the motion as to his intent and purpose. The presiding officer should rule frivolous and dilatory motions out of order.

When a motion is made, the presiding officer without asking for a second, should either state the motion or rule it out of order. This procedure will also eliminate the necessity of remembering which motions require a second and which do not.

In summary, with regard to seconding of motions:

1. The presiding officer normally states the motion without asking for a second.

2. Seconding of motions is eliminated in order to (a) avoid an unnecessary complication, (b) save time, (c) remove an unwise deterrent to the making of motions, and (d) lessen the temptation to debate a motion before making it.

Presence of a Quorum

A *quorum* is usually defined as the minimal number of members of a parliamentary body who are eligible to vote and who must be present in order to conduct business legally. The number constituting a quorum is defined in the bylaws; otherwise, common sense and common law usually define a quorum as a majority of the members of an organization. For a mass meeting that does not have the status of an organization, a quorum is the number present at the meeting.

It is the responsibility of the presiding officer to determine the presence of a quorum. He usually does this by checking quickly on the number of members present or by asking the secretary, parliamentarian, or another member to report to him on the status of a quorum. If the count is close, the presiding officer should announce the presence of a quorum as he opens the meeting, to reassure doubting members on this point. It is also the responsibility of the presiding officer to determine the presence of a quorum in the course of a meeting if he believes one no longer exists because members have left —the situation known as a "disappearing quorum." If a quorum is no longer present, the presiding officer must either close the meeting or limit the group to those actions permissible in the absence of a quorum. These actions are discussed below.)

If a quorum is not present when it is time to begin the meeting, the presiding officer should wait a few minutes to see if more members arrive. If a quorum does not convene, and it is already ten or fifteen minutes past the scheduled opening time, the presiding officer should announce the absence of a quorum and state that, unless a quorum can be rounded up, any business transacted (with the few exceptions to be noted later) will be unofficial and invalid. He should firmly resist suggestions by members that they proceed with the agenda in the hope that a quorum may later appear.

Among the valid actions which may be taken by an organization in the absence of a quorum are to adjourn, to take a recess, to set a time for the next meeting, or to take action to secure a quorum. It may also hear committee reports (but take no action on them), listen to remarks by members and others, and take emergency action if necessary, in the hope that such action will be approved at a later meeting with a quorum present.

If there is no quorum at a required meeting, such as one scheduled in the bylaws, the absence of a quorum does not invalidate compliance with the rules. The meeting was held, quorum or no quorum, and need not be rescheduled to comply with the requirement of a legal meeting. The meeting is legal; the conduct of most business without a quorum is not.

Organizations tend to set quorums too high. A quorum should be no larger than the number of members that might normally be expected to attend regularly scheduled meetings. Varying seasonal attendance and transportation problems in unfavorable weather should both be taken into account. Members who attend a meeting at some personal sacrifice of time and money feel justifiably disappointed and frustrated at the absence of a quorum.

This vexing problem is not limited to voluntary organizations. The United States House of Representatives adjourned once in 1966 and once in

1968 for want of a quorum; the United States Senate adjourned once in 1968 for the same reason. In both the House and the Senate, members may appear in the chambers to answer to their names and be included in the quorum count, and then leave. After trying for two hours and fifteen minutes to get enough members to answer for a quorum, Senate Democratic leader Mike Mansfield adjourned the Senate on September 24, 1968 when he finally secured the fifty-first member for a quorum, to find that only fifteen Senators were actually present.

There is no universally applicable rule for determining the number for a quorum. Each organization must judge what is best for its particular situation. In an organization with actively interested members from a contiguous area, a quorum of one-half of the members may present no problem. In an organization of similar size characterized by less active interest on the part of members and dull, sometimes unnecessary meetings, a quorum of ten percent may be too high.

Selecting the number for a quorum is a matter of good judgment. A quorum set too high may discourage attendance for fear a quorum may not convene, and one set too low may permit an unrepresentative minority to take advantage of the membership.

A quorum for a committee should usually be not less than one-half the committee's membership. However, in a committee which takes no binding actions, simply recommending actions to the assembly, it may be wise to set the quorum at less than a majority, or even to specify that those present constitute a quorum. Organizations should state in their bylaws the requirements for a quorum, including that for standing committees; otherwise, a quorum is assumed to be a majority of the membership.

It should be emphasized that attendance at meetings, and therefore the presence of a quorum, varies with the content of meetings. Members cannot be expected to attend meetings that are perfunctory and lack interest. Unless there is a genuine need for a meeting, it should

Modern Parliamentary Procedure

be canceled, with provisions for cancellation clearly outlined in the bylaws. On the other hand, the presiding officer and other officers should share the responsibility of adequate preparations for necessary meetings. The preparations should include the distribution in advance of a clearly worded agenda, including the names of any guest speakers; arrangements for visual presentations, if desirable; advance provision of a good public address system, and of comfortable lighting and ventilation in an area relatively free from disturbing noises.

To summarize, a quorum is essential for official business to be conducted, that is, for action to be taken on the meeting's agenda, with certain exceptions. It is the duty of the presiding officer to determine the presence of a quorum before opening the meeting. It is also the duty of any member, including the presiding officer, to question the presence of a quorum if he believes it is lacking, even if the meeting began with a quorum. The question of a "disappearing quorum" may be raised at any time, except to interrupt a speaker; a member rises and, without necessarily waiting for recognition from the presiding officer, states, "Mr. Chairperson, I question the presence of a quorum." The presiding officer must then determine if a quorum is present. If a quorum is obviously present, the presiding officer should consider repeated calls to determine the presence of a quorum dilatory, and hence out of order.

The question of the presence of a quorum must be raised immediately after a vote is taken for the absence of a quorum to invalidate that vote. "Immediately after" means prior to consideration of the next item on the agenda, or of any new subject, whether or not it is on the agenda. It is too late to invalidate an action after intervening business has been conducted, even if the absence of a quorum is then determined. The law presumes the continuing presence of a quorum if the meeting begins with one, and regards all actions taken as legal unless evidence clearly shows the absence of a quorum at the time of voting.

Main and Ordinary Motions

4

Main and
Ordinary Motions

A *main motion* is the statement of a request for action, an idea for evaluation, or the introduction of a *resolution* stating the group's position on a subject. It should be uncomplicated, as clear and concise as possible, and stated in the affirmative since the negative form is likely to result in confusion in voting. The presiding officer should request rephrasing of a motion if necessary to improve its clarity, or he may himself suggest a rephrased version for the approval of the proposer.

Consideration of a main motion may be the reason a meeting is held. The principal business of the meeting may be to determine the opinion of the assembly on the motion and to translate this judgment, when necessary, into a formal commitment by the assembly.

It is debatable (D); it may be amended (A); it almost always requires a majority vote (M) to pass; and the vote on it may be reconsidered (R). It is usually in order at any time there is no other main motion under consideration.

A main motion is usually a declarative statement, introduced by the expression, "I move that. . . ." For example:

I move that we donate twenty dollars to the Red Cross.

The Main Motion
Definition and Purpose

Requirements (D,A,M,R)

Forms and Examples

I move that we attend church this Sunday as a group.

I move that we purchase the property on South Street.

I move that we appoint a committee to investigate and to recommend the feasibility of our purchasing group insurance.

Discussion   A main motion may take the more ceremonious form of a resolution, presented in writing. In a resolution, a series of introductory clauses beginning "Whereas . . ." precede the action clause, which begins, "Now, therefore, be it resolved that . . ." Once a resolution is presented and accepted for consideration by the assembly, it is handled just like any other main motion.

A main motion in the form of a resolution is often used to express an organization's formal position on an issue, or to set forth an opinion in detail. It should be worked out carefully before the meeting, perhaps by several interested people willing to collaborate to find the right wording. It is a mistake to try to perfect the resolution under the pressure of an impatiently waiting assembly.

Resolved that this association express its appreciation to the retiring secretary, Mrs. Helen Brown, for her long years of faithful and efficient service.

Longer, more formal resolutions, usually beginning with a preamble (a series of Whereas clauses), should take the following form:

Whereas, The . . . and,
Whereas, The . . . and,
Whereas, The . . . , therefore be it
Resolved, That . . . ; and
Resolved, That . . .

To prevent confusion, only one main motion may be considered at a time. While its usual form is as illustrated above, there are some special motions and some ordinary motions that are handled as main motions. These include:

1. To Reconsider a vote
2. To Rescind a previous action
3. To Amend a motion already adopted
4. To Amend the bylaws
5. To Appeal, if offered when no motion is pending
6. To Recess, if offered when nothing else is pending or if qualified
7. To Adjourn, if qualified, such as including a time for adjournment in the motion, or if adjournment is moved without providing for another meeting.

These motions are discussed further in the appropriate sections below.

A main motion is debatable and amendable, and *Summary* its consideration may be referred to a committee or postponed; it usually requires only a majority vote to pass; the vote on it may be reconsidered; and the action taken, under most circumstances, may later be rescinded. Resolutions are main motions, usually more formal in structure and presented in written form, which set forth a position or opinion.

An amendment is a change in the wording of an **Ordinary Motions** amendable motion, usually a main motion, to To Amend make it express more accurately what the majority *Definition and Purpose* wants it to say, before it is voted on.

To Amend is debatable (D), amendable (A), and *Requirements (D,A,M)* requires a majority vote (M) to pass. The special meaning of "amendable" in this case is explained on page 43.

An amendment requires only a majority vote to pass, even if a two-thirds vote is required to pass the motion amended, as in the case of To Limit (Extend the Limits of) Debate, or To Amend a proposed change in the bylaws. When proposed on a debatable motion, amendments may have applied to them the motions To Limit or To Close Debate, and To Withdraw from consideration. A proposed amendment to a nondebatable motion, however, such as To Limit (Extend the Limits of) Debate, is not debatable.

A proposed amendment may not be separated from the motion it amends. Therefore, it may not *by itself*, be referred to a committee, nor its consideration postponed to another time.

Forms and Examples The exact change proposed, and its location in the motion, should be accurately specified. Some recommended forms follow:

1. I move *to delete* all after "Tuesday morning" in the motion.

2. I move to amend *by striking* the word "four" *and inserting* for it the word "six" in the motion.

3. I move *to add* to the motion the words "at the discretion of the President."

4. I move *to insert* the words "compact model" between the words "four" and "automobiles," making the passage read, if adopted, "the authorization for purchase of four *compact model* automobiles."

5. I move to amend *by substituting* for the motion "that we donate twenty-five dollars to the Christmas Fund" the following motion; "that the Treasurer send a check for fifty dollars to the local welfare office to assist needy families at Christmas."

Discussion The following ordinary motions may be amended:
1. To Amend—if the change proposed is accepted without formal motion and vote
2. To Refer—as to size of committee, selection process, deadline for report, conditions of referral, etc.
3. To Postpone—as to the limits of postponement.

4. To Limit (Extend the Limits of) Debate
—as to number of speakers, etc.
5. To Recess—as to duration of recess.

The process of further modifying a proposed amendment to a main motion deserves special attention. Members must be free to effect as many changes in a motion as are required to make it state accurately the wishes of the assembly. The procedure for change should be easy for the average person to follow. For this reason, the confusing and redundant To Amend the Amendment is dropped as a parliamentary motion.

This does not mean that it is impossible to amend an amendment. It means either that suggested changes in a proposed amendment are accepted without a formal vote, or that the originally proposed amendment is voted on first and the suggested change to it is offered later as another proposed amendment. Thus, *only one proposed amendment is pending at a time*.

An experienced presiding officer will have little difficulty with this procedure. In most cases, a suggested change in a proposed amendment may be incorporated simply by the presiding officer's asking permission of the mover of the original amendment. If the suggested change is of questionable merit in the minds of some members, perhaps including the presiding officer, and unacceptable to the mover of the original amendment, the presiding officer may state, "After the proposed amendment is voted on, opportunities will be given to present other suggestions as separate amendments," and proceed with discussion of the pending amendment.

In brief, changes in a proposed amendment are agreed to informally, or by general consent if requested by the presiding officer; if the proposed change is not accepted in this fashion, it can be offered later for separate consideration. In this limited sense, proposed amendments may be further amended.

This procedure eliminates the confusing term Amending the Amendment, a term that should not be used even in the informal consideration of a requested change. Instead, one should refer specifically to the proposed change; there is no need to label it.

This procedure is already used by hundreds of small groups under, say, forty members. And it should always be used by groups of only ten to fifteen and by committees. In meetings of large organizations, the presiding officer's skill in human relations may be challenged by this approach, but the overall simplification is well worth it. In practically all cases, it saves time otherwise required for formal consideration and vote on the "secondary amendment," as it has been called. Even if a suggested change in a proposed amendment is later put to a vote as a proposed amendment itself, this process does not make necessary any more votes than would have been required To Amend the Amendment. Of course, any number of proposed changes germane to an amendment may be accepted before putting the revised form to a vote.

A special form of amending called *Filling Blanks* is a timesaving device that may be used to resolve questions when several options are in need of consideration at the same time. This may involve deciding on an amount of money, a name, a preferred date or time, and the like, to be included in a proposed amendment to a motion. It can also be used, particularly in small groups, to secure group preference for one of several possible items or forms of wording for inclusion in the initial statement of a motion.

An example may help. Suppose a motion to send a delegate to the annual convention is under consideration, and the discussion centers on who would go if the motion were passed. Several names are mentioned. A blank might be created by amending the motion to delete the words "a delegate," with the understanding that the blank will be filled by vote. If four or five members are nominated, the group votes for or against each, in the order nominated, and the name of the person receiving the highest affirmative vote is entered to fill the blank. Discussion continues on the main motion.

This is a form of amending a motion. Of course, the motion discussed above could initially have been introduced with a blank to be filled by vote of the members. An alert presiding officer, seeing multiple choices presented that need consideration in changing a motion, may suggest, "If there is no objection, the choice will be determined after the manner of filling blanks."

Amendments proposed to a main motion should be germane—that is, closely related—and appropriate to the motion to warrant consideration. An amendment should not be used to change an affirmative proposal of action into a negative proposal *not* to take that action. An amendment should not be at odds with the general intent of the main motion, although it may be hostile to the proposed method of fulfilling the intent of the main motion.

It is sometimes difficult for the presiding officer to decide whether or not to accept a proposed amendment. When in doubt, the presiding officer is advised to ask the assembly if there is objection to considering the proposal as an amendment. If a member objects, a vote should be taken. A majority vote in favor of consideration would be required. Because this decision would be made by the assembly, no appeal could be entertained on it. No amount of effort at defining what is germane can take the place of common sense on the part of the presiding officer and the assembly in determining whether a proposed amendment should be considered.

In the case of a *substitute motion*—that is, a motion replacing the main motion—proposed as an amendment, the procedure outlined above is followed. If entertained as germane, informal changes in the amendment are permitted; if the vote on the substitute amendment carries, the original main motion is replaced by it; and the new main motion may be further amended before a vote is taken to approve or reject it.[1]

When a main motion with a proposed amendment pending is referred to a committee, the proposed amendment remains attached. It is considered again when the motion is reintroduced to the assembly, perhaps with a committee's recommendation on the wisdom of adopting the proposed amendment. The same course is followed when To Postpone the consideration of a main motion and its proposed amendment is passed by an assembly.

To amend a motion previously passed is a main motion, and is handled like any other main motion. It is debatable, amendable, and requires a majority vote to pass. However, no motion previously passed may be amended by a lesser vote than was required to pass the main motion originally. Thus, a motion that required a two-thirds vote to pass may not be amended by less than a two-thirds vote.

Access to a main motion previously voted on is also possible via the motion To Reconsider, provided the vote was taken in the same session. A proposed amendment to a bylaw is a main motion. It usually requires previous notice of intent to amend and a two-thirds vote to pass, depending on the provisions included in the bylaws.

[1]This eliminates a complicated procedure that permits a substitute motion to be entertained as a *primary* amendment, and a second substitute called a *secondary* amendment considered on, first the original motion and then to the substitute motion, before voting on the substitute motion. And when a committee reports on a motion—that had proposed primary and secondary amendments pending when it was referred to the committee—by recommending a substitute motion for the original main motion, the situation invites confusion. The terms primary and secondary relating to amendments are used in *Robert's Rules of Order Newly Revised* (Glenview, Ill.: Scott, Foresman and Company, 1970), pp. 129–135, 436–439. On page 111 Robert states that he prefers these terms over saying "amendments of the first [second] degree," although all are accurate designations. It is surprising that Sturgis (*Sturgis Standard Code of Parliamentary Procedure*, 2nd ed. [New York: McGraw-Hill, 1966], p. 54) would permit three proposed amendments, the proposed substitute motion and "amendments of both ranks" to it, to be pending at once.

A main motion may be amended as many times as the assembly wishes, but only one proposed amendment may be considered at a time. A proposed amendment may be modified by general agreement, or by consent of the mover of the proposed amendment, as many times as the group wishes before putting it to a vote.

The motion To Refer is almost always used to send the consideration of a main motion to a committee. The most frequent use of To Refer is to permit a smaller group of selected, more knowledgeable members to give a motion detailed consideration and to report their findings back to the parent group. To refer a motion to a hostile committee in order to kill it is not a legitimate use of referral.

To Refer
Definition and Purpose

The motion to refer to a committee is debatable (D), and may be amended (A) as to the number on the committee, the selection process, instructions to the committee, the deadline and instructions for reporting. It often saves time to include this information in the wording of the original motion To Refer. Referral to a standing committee need not include this information, since it has probably already been written into the bylaws. The motion To Refer requires a majority vote (M) to pass. The vote on a motion To Refer may not be reconsidered, since the motion may be renewed in the same meeting.

Requirements (D,A,M)

The simplest form is:

Forms and Examples

I move we refer this motion to a committee.

It is preferable to state the motion as follows:

I move we refer the consideration of the motion that [stating the motion] to a committee of three, appointed by the chair, to report at our next meeting.

Discussion   Chapter 8 discusses the functions of a committee, the selection of and duties of members, procedure in meetings, committee reports, and so forth.

Summary   The motion To Refer is debatable; it may be amended or withdrawn; it requires a majority vote; and it is in order if a proposed amendment is pending, but not if other motions ranking above it are pending (except by Suspending the Rules). If the motion fails, it may be renewed after further discussion; and debate on it may be limited or closed to expedite a decision. To Refer to a committee a subject not pending, or to appoint a committee to do a particular task not under consideration as a motion, is a main motion, treated like any other main motion.

To Postpone

Definition and Purpose   The motion To Postpone, if passed, removes a subject from consideration until the time or meeting specified in the motion To Postpone. Its purpose may be to set aside temporarily the consideration of a motion to permit consideration of more pressing business; to delay consideration and action until a more appropriate time; or to allow time for the development of a consensus or for caucusing, and so forth.

Requirements (D,A,M)   To Postpone is debatable (D); may be amended (A) as to the time or conditions of postponement; and requires a majority vote (M) to pass. It applies to main motions only. It may have applied to it motions To Limit (Extend the Limits of) Debate, To Close Debate, or To Withdraw. A vote on the ordinary motion To Postpone may not be reconsidered, since the motion may be renewed in the same meeting.

Forms and Examples   1.   I move To Postpone this motion for fifteen minutes to permit the assembly to greet Senator Williams, who has just arrived.

2. I move To Postpone until our next regular meeting the consideration of the motion that we purchase a station wagon for our organization.

3. I move To Postpone consideration of the pending main motion until we have heard the quarterly report from the Committee on Finances.

Discussion

When one speaks of postponing a motion, it is technically, of course, the *consideration of the motion* that is postponed, not the motion itself. If the consideration of a motion is postponed until another meeting, the secretary lists it under "Unfinished Business" on the *agenda* for that meeting. To Postpone consideration of a motion until meaningful action is impossible, in order to kill the motion, is not a proper use of the motion To Postpone. A motion To Postpone consideration by referring to a committee is stated by the presiding officer as a motion To Refer to a committee, not To Postpone.

When postponement is suggested to permit consideration of a more pressing matter, or to deal with an emergency situation such as the unexpected arrival of a dignitary, the motion should specify that the pending business be postponed until the other matter has been resolved. The motion thus postponed is returned to consideration at the appropriate time by the presiding officer, who states the motion and declares that it is again open for discussion, under exactly the same conditions as before it was postponed. Used in this fashion, the motion To Postpone includes the function of the obsolete motion To Lay on the Table, discussed in Chapter 6.

Summary

To Postpone ranks above the motions To Amend and To Refer. Thus, if a motion To Amend or To Refer is pending, the motion To Postpone is in order, but neither of these motions is in order if a motion To Postpone is pending (except by Suspending the Rules). To Postpone is not in order if motions of higher rank—To Limit (Extend the Limits of) Debate, To Close Debate, To Recess, and To Adjourn—are pending (except by Suspending the Rules). Proposed amendments to the main motion are postponed if consideration of the main motion is postponed. A motion To Refer is ignored if pending when a motion To Postpone is passed.

To Limit (Extend the Limits of) Debate
Definition and Purpose

The purpose of the motion is to permit an assembly to control discussion of a motion by setting limits on the time allowable for discussion before voting on the pending motion.

Requirements (A, 2/3)

To Limit (Extend the Limits of) Debate, in either of its forms, is not debatable. It is amendable (A), as to the specific time limits involved, but these proposed amendments are not themselves debatable. Since To Limit Debate may infringe on the basic principle of freedom of discussion, a two-thirds vote (2/3) is required to pass. The vote may not be reconsidered, since the motion may be renewed in the same meeting. It is in order when any debatable motion is pending, but not, of course, when To Recess or To Adjourn is pending. Limitations on debate imposed by passing the motion To Limit Debate are not valid beyond the meeting or convention in which they were authorized. The effect of To Limit (Extend the Limits of) Debate ceases to apply when a motion is referred or postponed.

Forms and Examples

1.   I move To Limit Debate on the motion that [stating the motion] to no more than thirty minutes.

2.   I move To Extend the Limits of Debate to one hour to permit more thorough discussion of this motion.

3.   I move To Limit Debate to three speakers for each side of the question, each to speak no longer than five minutes.

Motions To Limit Debate are implemented by the presiding officer who announces when the limit has been exhausted, and proceeds to call for a vote on the immediately pending motion. If a group has decided to limit debate on a main motion to, say, thirty minutes, such other motions as To Refer and To Postpone may be made during this thirty-minute period; if one of these other motions should pass, the motion to limit debate is invalidated. During the thirty-minute period, the assembly may also vote To Recess (the recess is not counted against the thirty minutes) or To Adjourn, ending the limit on debate.

Motions To Limit Debate or To Extend the Limits of Debate may be amended only as to the specific time limit or number of speakers involved. Proposed amendments are not debatable. Neither form admits of debate, and both require a two-thirds vote to pass. The motion To Limit Debate is in order when any debatable motion is pending, and yields only to the ordinary motions To Recess and To Adjourn. To Limit (Extend the Limits of) Debate and To Close Debate are the only ordinary motions requiring a two-thirds vote, because they potentially curb a member's freedom of discussion.

Discussion

Summary

When a motion To Close Debate is passed, all discussion on the pending motion (or motions) is terminated, and the assembly proceeds to vote on the immediately pending motion, unless a motion of higher rank, such as To Adjourn, intervenes.

To Close Debate

Definition and Purpose

To Close Debate is not debatable, and requires a two-thirds vote (2/3) to pass.[2] It is not amendable

Requirements (2/3)

[2]According to Paul Mason (*Mason's Manual of Legislative Procedure* [New York: McGraw-Hill, 1953], p. 115) however, only a majority vote is necessary to close debate in *legislative* bodies. Organizations could control debate by majority vote if they adopted a rule of order to that effect. Most authorities, however, believe a two-thirds vote should be required to close debate.

in the usual sense but, by general consent, its form may be changed to make it applicable not only to the immediately pending motion but also to other pending debatable motions, or vice versa. Its consideration may not be postponed or referred to a committee, and a vote on it may not be reconsidered. Like all motions it may, of course, be withdrawn from consideration before voting. It may not be applied to undebatable motions.[3]

Its usual form is "To Close Debate on [stating the pending motion]." It may be applied to any main motion and to the ordinary motions To Amend, To Refer, and To Postpone, as well as to the debatable special motions To Appeal, To Reconsider, and To Rescind. When so moved and carried by a two-thirds vote, its effect is to bring to an immediate vote the motion on which it was moved. After that vote has been taken, its effect has been exhausted.

Another form of the motion, however, is permissible. A member may move "To Close Debate on all pending motions." If, for example, a main motion, a motion To Amend, and a motion To Postpone were pending, a favorable vote To Close Debate on all pending motions would require votes on all three motions, starting with the last motion made. That is, the assembly would vote first on To Postpone consideration of the main motion, then on the motion To Amend the main motion, and finally on the main motion itself, perhaps as amended. If the first vote passes, of course, consideration of the main motion and the proposed amendment would be postponed and the effect of closure of debate would be exhausted. If the vote on To Postpone were negative, the assembly would proceed to vote on the proposed amendment and, regardless of the out-

[3]In what appears to be an unnecessarily complicated device *Robert's Rules of Order Newly Revised* (pp. 162, 198) permits the motion To Close Debate (The Previous Question) to be applied to the undebatable motions To Limit (Extend the Limits of) Debate and To Recess for the purpose of preventing amendments to these amendable motions.

Modern Parliamentary Procedure

come of that vote, go on directly to vote on the main motion. Further motions To Amend, To Refer, and To Postpone may not be presented while the motion To Close Debate is still in effect.

1. I move To Close Debate (understood to apply only to the immediately pending motion).

2. I move To Close Debate on all pending debatable motions (applicable to the main motion, a proposed amendment, To Refer, and To Postpone, depending on what is pending when To Close Debate is moved).

3. I move To Close Debate on the motions, To Postpone, and To Refer (that is, not to include the proposed amendment and the main motion within the scope of To Close Debate.)

Forms and Examples

The motion To Close Debate should be used infrequently. Too frequent use of this motion may reflect unfavorably on the presiding officer's skill in handling a group; or it may be symptomatic of factional dissension within a group, or of attempted misuse of parliamentary strategy to prohibit information unfavorable to the motion from being revealed. It should not be entertained by the presiding officer (whose decision may be appealed and reversed) if a fair opportunity to discuss the motion has not been given to all interested members.

Discussion

For two or three members to speak for or against a motion and then move To Close Debate is a travesty of parliamentary procedure, if members who have not yet been heard are trying to present their views. Of course, it is out of order for a member to move To Close Debate at the conclusion of his own remarks, or to include it in a motion he presents for consideration. However, when a small group insists on prolonging debate, perhaps intentionally delaying a vote by talking beyond the scheduled time for adjournment —that is, *filibustering*—To Close Debate allows two-thirds of those voting to stop such dilatory tactics and bring the pending motion to a vote.

Summary A motion To Close Debate may be applied to any debatable motion. It may be applicable to the immediately pending motion only, or to some or all pending debatable motions. When passed in the latter form, it prevents motions To Postpone, To Refer, or To Amend from being offered, and requires that votes be taken on all motions to which To Close Debate is applicable. If a motion To Refer or To Postpone is pending when debate is ordered closed on all pending motions, an affirmative vote on either To Refer or To Postpone removes the main motion from immediate consideration and cancels further application to it of the motion To Close Debate. This does not apply, however, when consideration of a motion is postponed only temporarily and resumed later in the same meeting. In this case the effect of the motion To Close Debate remains applicable to the main motion when consideration is resumed.

To Recess
Definition and Purpose To Recess is a motion to interrupt a meeting. Its purpose is often to provide a brief rest period in a tiring session, to continue a meeting to another day, to break for a specific purpose (count ballots, refreshments) while also stipulating a definite time to reconvene the meeting.

Requirements (A,M) To Recess is not debatable; it may be amended (A) as to the time limit of the recess; and it requires a majority vote (M) to pass. Although the motion is not debatable, the mover of the motion To Recess, or of a proposed amendment to it, should be permitted to state his reason for offering the motion or amendment.

To Recess is in order provided the motion To Adjourn is not pending, since To Recess ranks above other ordinary motions and is outranked only by the motion To Adjourn. Proposed amendments to the motion To Recess are not debatable, and they must be limited in subject to the length of time of the recess, or the specific times when it is to begin and end. A vote on the ordinary motion To Recess may not be reconsidered, since the motion may be offered again in the same meeting.

Forms and Examples

1. I move we recess for ten minutes.

2. I move we recess until the speaker arrives.

3. I move we recess until ten o'clock in the morning (applicable in a convention, for example, at which the session consists of a series of meetings, and the motion To Recess, if passed, does not adjourn the convention).

4. I move we recess until the ballots have been canvassed.

5. By the presiding officer: If there is no objection, we shall recess for refreshments, reconvening at 10:45 A.M. (If there is no objection, the recess begins immediately.)

Discussion

A recess begins immediately on passing the motion To Recess. If a recess is announced in official agenda or a program, the presiding officer declares the recess in effect when the announced time arrives, and reconvenes the assembly at the expiration of the recess. No motions are required to effect these actions.

If made when there is no main motion pending, or if it provides for a recess to be taken at a later time, To Recess is a main motion, handled like any other main motion. When offered while a main motion is under consideration, however, To Recess ranks just below To Adjourn and is not debatable.

The motion To Recess must stipulate the duration of the recess, and thus provide for reconvening the meeting. There is no limit on the length of a recess, as long as it neither extends beyond the time set for the next regular or special meeting nor constitutes an adjournment, as in a convention. The motion To Recess is in order as a main motion in the absence of a quorum, and may be used to await the presence of a quorum.

Summary To Recess provides for an interval in the meeting, not an adjournment. It may be conveniently used when waiting for a speaker to arrive, ballots to be canvassed, or the room to be ventilated, or for a coffee break or brief cooling-off period in a heated discussion, and so forth. Little difficulty is normally encountered by the motion To Recess. To Recess may have applied to it only the motions To Amend and To Withdraw. When the presiding officer calls the meeting to order following a recess, the group resumes its considerations at the point at which it was interrupted.

To Adjourn
Definition and Purpose

Adjournment is the termination of a meeting or convention session, with the next meeting to be held following a new call for a meeting. When offered and passed in any but the last of a series of meetings in a convention, it should be recorded as a motion To Recess, not To Adjourn, since only the termination of the last meeting in a convention is, technically, an adjournment.

Requirements (M)

To Adjourn is the highest-ranking ordinary motion. When not qualified in any way, and when made while a main motion is under consideration, it is neither debatable nor amendable and requires a majority vote to pass. It is in order at any time after a meeting has convened, provided the mover has been recognized by the presiding officer and does not interrupt a speaker or interfere with the taking or counting of a vote. It would not be in order if a motion To Adjourn had just been defeated and no intervening business had been introduced.

A vote on the ordinary motion To Adjourn may not be reconsidered, since it may be renewed in the same meeting after any intervening business has been introduced. To Adjourn is in order as a main motion in the absence of a quorum.

1. I move that we adjourn. (When other business is pending, this is a nondebatable, nonamendable motion requiring a majority vote to pass.)

2. I move that we adjourn until April 17 at 4:00 P.M. (If the time specified is that scheduled for the next regular meeting, this form merely constitutes a reminder, and the motion is limited as in number 1.)

3. I move that we adjourn until April 17 at 4:00 P.M. (If the time specified represents a previously unscheduled meeting, the motion is a main motion, in order only if no other main motion is pending, debatable, and amendable.

4. (By the presiding officer, when a time for adjournment has been previously fixed by an adopted rule, program, or motion:) The time set for adjournment has arrived. The chair is willing to entertain a motion To Adjourn.

    or

    Since our fixed time for adjournment has arrived, if there is no objection, the meeting is adjourned.

To Adjourn is the highest-ranking ordinary motion. Under normal circumstances, nothing can prevent a majority of an assembly from terminating a meeting. If the agenda for a meeting has been completed and no one wants the floor, the presiding officer should adjourn the meeting by announcing, "Since there is no further business, if there is no objection the meeting is adjourned." This is a legitimate procedure, implying a vote by general consent. No meeting is legally adjourned until the presiding officer *announces* the adjournment following a vote on the motion, whether counted or by general consent.

The presiding officer should not put the motion To Adjourn to a vote before making such necessary announcements as the time and place of the next meeting. In fact, in between taking a vote on To Adjourn and announcing the results of the vote, the presiding officer may give this information. If business must be considered after the presiding officer has entertained a motion To Adjourn, he may request permission to withdraw the motion, or, having explained the urgency of the situation, may state, "The chair requests that this urgent matter be attended to before adjournment" and proceed to state the question.

A motion To Adjourn to an Adjourned Meeting—that is, to continue a meeting at another set time—should be handled as is a motion To Recess; and this eliminates the confusing terminology of the other motion. The limitations imposed on the motion To Recess would, of course, apply.

What happens to the unfinished business of an organization when it adjourns? In an organization whose meetings are scheduled quarterly, monthly, or weekly, items on the agenda not covered before adjournment are carried forward to the next meeting as unfinished business. In organizations whose scheduled meetings are less frequent, all items on the agenda not covered when the meeting is adjourned are dropped. If they are included in the agenda for the next meeting, they are not listed as unfinished business.

When a meeting is continued to a time not representing a regularly scheduled meeting to permit the agenda to be covered, the motion To Recess is appropriate; the agenda is resumed at the exact point at which it was interrupted by the motion To Recess. An example is the prolonged consideration of extensive changes in a group's bylaws. Several meetings may be required, with perhaps as little as a day or a week between meetings, to complete consideration of the proposed amendments. In such successive meetings, the group should begin where it left off at the previous meeting.

To Adjourn, when unqualified, is the highest- *Summary* ranking ordinary motion; it is neither debatable nor amendable and requires a majority vote to pass. When it is qualified in any way, it is handled like any other main motion. Official adjournment takes place only when the presiding officer announces the results of a majority affirmative vote, counted or by general consent, on the motion To Adjourn.

Special Motions

5

Special Motions

A Point of Order is the procedure followed to call the attention of the presiding officer to a violation of the rules, an omission or a mistake in the proceedings, or any unusual situation requiring immediate attention. Its purpose is to provide a means for a member to secure a ruling from the chair on a matter thought to be of sufficient importance to require immediate attention.

A Point of Order is not debatable, not amendable, and requires no vote since the presiding officer decides the point at issue. It is in order at any time. The presiding officer should decide on the basis of its urgency whether it requires immediate action. One may interrupt a speaker to raise a Point of Order. That a Point of Order is not debatable should not prevent the member who raises it from explaining his position or the presiding officer from stating his position in ruling on the request.

1. Member: Madam Chairwoman, I rise to a Point of Order.
   Chair: State your point.
   Member: We have two main motions on the floor.
   Chair: Your point is well taken. We shall consider only [stating the motion] at this time.

   or

Point of Order
Definition and Purpose

Requirements

Forms and Examples

The only main motion now under consideration is [stating the motion]. Therefore, your point is not well taken.

2. Member: I rise to a Point of Order.
    Chair: State your point.
    Member: We can't hear the speaker.
    Chair: Will the speaker please speak up so he can be heard?

3. Member: Mr. President, I rise to a Point of Order.
    Chair: State your point.
    Member: I resent the insulting language of the speaker and his insinuations about the motives of members who support the motion.
    Chair: Your point is well taken. The speaker will please be more temperate in his language and will please confine his discussion to the merits of the proposal and not question the integrity of members.

Discussion   A member may appeal the ruling of the presiding officer to the assembly, following the procedure outlined in the next section. On the other hand, if the presiding officer is in doubt about the proper response to a Point of Order, he may refer the decision to the assembly for a decision by majority vote. There is no appeal from a decision of the assembly on a Point of Order.

A Point of Order is not a motion at all, but the protected privilege of a member to call the presiding officer's attention to something. Technically, a Point of Order is raised to inform the presiding officer of an infraction of the rules and to demand that proper procedure be followed, when further delay would only compound the error. It is sometimes used, however, for requests unrelated to infractions of the rules: A member may rise to a Point of Order to state that the room is too hot, that he can't hear the speaker, or simply to ask a question regarding proper parliamentary procedure. Such requests may properly be considered points of order if the implied rights of members are being violated. For example, a member has the right to have reasonable provision made for his comfort, and to hear what is being said. These requests are not technically Points of Order, but they can be handled as such by the presiding officer in less time than it takes to explain the minor procedural variation involved, and the presiding officer should do so. The abuse of such requests is, of course, harmful, but rules alone cannot prevent it.

The Point of Order may be used in any of the following circumstances:

1. To question the validity of the parliamentary procedure being followed (as in Example 1)
2. To call a speaker to order for the inappropriate use of language or another breach of decorum (as in Example 3)
3. To call attention to a condition that inconveniences members (as in Example 2)
4. To raise a parliamentary inquiry, or to call attention to a violation of correct procedure
5. To question a ruling by the presiding officer on a point of parliamentary procedure prior to appealing his decision to the judgment of the assembly.

Summary

A Point of Order should only be used for urgent situations. It is a method of drawing the immediate attention of the presiding officer and the assembly to a pressing problem. If a member has overestimated the urgency of his Point of Order, the chairman may state that he will answer it later when to do so would not interrupt a speaker. A ruling on the part of the presiding officer may be appealed by any member to the judgment of the assembly. Appeals may not be made on points involving the correctness of procedures since their accuracy may be checked by consulting the rules. The presiding officer's opinion about a rule does not constitute a ruling.

Definition and Purpose

To Appeal the ruling of the presiding officer means to subject his ruling to examination by the assembly and to secure its support or reversal of the ruling. The purpose of this motion is to monitor the appropriateness and accuracy of the presiding officer's rulings and to prevent the arbitrary exercise of power.

Requirements (D,M)

To Appeal is debatable (D), and may not be amended, postponed, or referred to a committee.

To be in order an appeal must be raised immediately after the ruling in question is made by the presiding officer; the mover may interrupt a speaker to do so. It may have applied to it the motions To Limit (Extend the Limits of) Debate, To Close Debate, and To Withdraw.

In putting an appeal to a vote, the question is always stated in such a way that the affirmative vote to support the ruling of the chair is requested first, followed by the negative vote to reverse the ruling by the chair. A majority vote (M) in the negative is required to overrule the ruling of the presiding officer; a tie vote sustains the ruling of the presiding officer.

If made when a main motion is not pending, the appeal becomes a main motion, and is treated accordingly.

Forms and Examples

1. Member: Ms. President, I appeal from the ruling of the chair that [stating the decision].

   Chair: The ruling of the chair that [stating the decision in question] has been appealed from. Will the member please state his reasons for appealing?

   Member: [States his reasons]

   Chair: [States reasons supporting his ruling] Is there other discussion on the motion? Are you ready to vote?

   Chair: Those in favor of accepting the ruling of the chair that [stating the

ruling] please hold up their right
hands. Thank you. Those opposed, the same sign. Thank you.
The ruling of the chair is upheld
by a vote of 21 to 9.

or

The ruling of the chair is reversed
by a vote of 10 in favor and 14
opposed, and the judgment of the
assembly is that [stating the
decision of the assembly].

2.   Member: Mr. Chairperson, I rise to a Point
of Order.

    Chair: Please state your point.

    Member: We have erred in permitting
amendments to the motion To
Limit Debate. This motion may
not be amended.

    Chair: Your point is not well taken. To
Limit Debate is amendable as to
time limitations and the amendments permitted were of
this type.

    Member: Mr. Chairperson, I appeal
from the ruling of the chair.

    Chair: Since this is not a ruling by the
chair, no appeal can be enter-
tained. Our adopted parliamentary authority, *Modern Parliamentary Procedure*, states on page 50
[reading the requirements for the
motion To Limit Debate].

3.   Member: Madam President, I appeal the
ruling of the chair made earlier
in this meeting that my proposed
amendment to the motion [stating
the motion] was not germane.

    Chair: Mr. Speaker, that main motion
has been disposed of: Therefore,
your appeal is out of order. To be
in order a motion To Appeal must
be offered immediately after the

ruling in question is made by the chair.

Discussion When a member wants to determine whether the presiding officer's ruling is consistent with the wishes of the assembly, he may appeal from the ruling of the chair. This procedure is often undertaken in response to the presiding officer's ruling on a Point of Order.

Care should be taken to appeal only *rulings* by the presiding officer. Appeals may not be made on accepted truths, known facts, existing laws, or established rules. That a main motion is debatable, for example, is not subject to appeal. The announcement of a vote or the answer to an inquiry on parliamentary procedure may not be appealed, since verification by other means is readily available. Any ruling involving the presiding officer's personal judgment or opinion, however, is subject to appeal, including such issues as whether or not a proposed amendment is germane or what constitutes misconduct on the part of members.

Summary An appeal permits any member to submit his doubts about the validity of a ruling by the chair to examination by the assembly. Since the appeal must be proposed immediately following the ruling in question, a member may interrupt a speaker to request an appeal. The appeal must be decided immediately on being requested.

To Withdraw
Definition and Purpose

To Withdraw a motion is to remove it from consideration. The purpose of To Withdraw is to provide a means for terminating consideration of a motion without actually voting on it. It permits abandonment of a motion whose consideration might prove embarrassing to the assembly. To Withdraw has been widened in scope to subsume the purpose and function of the motion To Postpone Indefinitely, discussed further in Chapter 6.

To Withdraw is not debatable, although the mover should be permitted to state his reasons. It is not amendable and requires a majority vote (M) to pass. A request To Withdraw a motion may, however, be granted by the chair without a vote, regardless of the stage of consideration the motion has reached. If there is objection, a vote may be taken "that the motion [stating the motion] be withdrawn." Any motion may be withdrawn; no other motion may be applied to the motion To Withdraw.

Requirements (M):

1. Member: Mr. President, I request permission To Withdraw my motion that [stating the motion].
   Chair: The motion that [stating the motion] is withdrawn.

2. Member: Ms. Chairwoman, I move that the motion that [stating the motion] be withdrawn from consideration.
   Chair: Please state your reasons for requesting the withdrawal of the motion.
   Member: A discussion of this motion will require revelation of the personal finances of some members of this organization, and will be embarrassing to them.
   Chair: Very well, if there is no objection . . .
   Member: I object, Ms. Chairwoman. The motion should be considered even if some members must give personal financial information.
   Chair: There has been objection to withdrawing the motion. Those in favor of withdrawing the motion that [stating the motion] please raise your right hands. Thank you. Those opposed to withdrawing? Thank you. The motion

Forms and Examples

To Withdraw has passed by a vote of 27 to 11, and the motion that [stating the motion] is withdrawn.

3. Member: Mr. Chairman, I request permission To Withdraw my motion that [stating the motion].

Chair: There is obvious interest in the motion, as evidenced by our discussion of the motion for the past thirty minutes. Please state your reasons for wanting To Withdraw it.

Member: I had no idea that some members felt so strongly on this motion, and I would like To Withdraw it to prevent further antagonisms from developing.

Chair: Very well, if there is no objection, the motion will be withdrawn.

Member: Mr. Chairman, I object to withdrawal of the motion.

Chair: There has been an objection to withdrawal of the motion. The motion is to grant the member permission to withdraw his motion. Those in favor of granting such permission, etc.

Discussion Before a motion has been stated by the presiding officer, the mover may withdraw it by stating, "I withdraw my motion." A motion may be withdrawn either by request of the mover or by a formal motion To Withdraw by any member at any time previous to the final vote on the motion. Withdrawal of a motion may be granted by the chairman, by general consent, or by a majority vote of the assembly. The effect of granting the withdrawal of a motion is the same as if the motion had never been proposed. Therefore, a withdrawn motion may be renewed, if appropriate, in the same or later meetings.

A motion that has been withdrawn after having been stated by the presiding officer is recorded by the secretary with a statement that it was withdrawn. The secretary does not record a withdrawn motion if it is withdrawn before being stated by the presiding officer.

Summary

The motion To Withdraw provides an assembly with a means to eliminate a motion without revealing how members stand on it. The motion may take the form of a request To Withdraw by the mover of a motion, or that of the more formal proposal by any member, "I move that the motion [stating the motion] be withdrawn."

To Suspend the Rules
Definition and Purpose

To Suspend the Rules is to set aside or make inoperative in a given situation a rule of order that would otherwise prevent the assembly from taking a desired action. Its purpose is to allow an organization to violate its own rules of procedure when the circumstances warrant.

Requirements (2/3)

To Suspend the Rules is not debatable, not amendable, and requires a two-thirds vote (2/3) to pass; the vote on it may not be reconsidered. When approved, it sets aside *temporarily* a rule of order to permit a particular action to be undertaken, and its effect expires when that action is completed.

Forms and Examples

1. Member: Madam Chairperson, I move To Suspend the Rules to hear the report of the Special Committee on Convention Planning before the regular standing committee reports.
   Chair: If there is no objection [pausing] the rules will be suspended to permit the report of the Special Committee on Convention Planning to be heard now. Will the chairperson of that committee please proceed with the committee report?

2. Member: Mr. President: I move To Sus-
                pend the Rules to consider items
                under Unfinished Business
                immediately.
    Chair: If there is no objection, we will go
                immediately to the first item
                under Unfinished Business on
                the agenda.
    Member: Mr. President, I object.
    Chair: There has been objection to the
                motion To Suspend the Rules. A
                two-thirds vote in favor of
                Suspending the Rules is required
                to change our rules of order
                governing the order of business.
                Those in favor of Suspending
                the Rules to permit taking up
                items under Unfinished Business
                immediately, please raise your
                right hands, etc.

3. Member: Madam President, I move we
                Suspend the Rule requiring a
                quorum so that we can get down
                to work.
    Chair: The rule stating that the presence
                of a quorum is necessary to
                conduct business legally may
                not be suspended. Therefore,
                the motion is out of order.

Discussion Only procedural rules may be suspended. These
may be either rules of order and standing rules
or procedural rules set forth in the adopted parliamentary authority. The distinction between
rules of order and standing rules is discussed in
Chapter 11. To Suspend the Rules does not apply
to bylaws. To avoid confusion on this point,
organizations should list rules of order and standing rules separately from bylaws.

Certain rules may not be suspended. Members
may not be deprived of their rights by suspending
the rules. Rules governing voting methods and
requirements, stipulating advance notice of a

meeting, governing the conditions for calling a meeting, or setting a quorum may not be suspended. While bylaws may not be suspended, if a rule of order is listed with the bylaws instead of separately, its location does not prevent its suspension by a two-thirds vote. The adopted parliamentary authority may not be suspended, though it may be changed by amending the bylaws.

On occasion an organization may wish to proceed in its deliberations in a way that violates its own rules of order or standing rules. For example, suppose that debate on a motion has been closed by the usual two-thirds vote, when the assembly suddenly becomes aware that the only real expert among the members on the issue in question has just arrived. By suspending the rule prohibiting debate on a motion when it has been ordered closed, the member may be heard. As soon as he has finished, however, the effect of the suspension of rules expires. In this instance, the presiding officer would probably request general consent to suspend the rule in question and, if there were no objection, call on the member to speak.

To Suspend the Rules is in order when a motion is pending, if its purpose is related to that motion. Suppose that during the reports of standing committees, the presiding officer of a special committee finds that he must leave the meeting before he would be called on to report in the normal order of business. For him to present his report early would violate a rule of order governing the order of business. He or any other member may move To Suspend the Rule requiring his report to be given in accordance with the order of business and "to permit the report to be heard now." If passed, the rule is suspended only for the duration of the report in question; procedure then reverts to the accepted order of business.

To Suspend the Rules is used infrequently, but occasions arise when it is needed as an orderly and acceptable way of accomplishing a specific

Summary

purpose. The vote on the motion To Suspend the Rules may be by general consent; if no one objects, the presiding officer announces that the rule in question has been set aside temporarily and proceeds to the matter now eligible to be brought to the attention of the assembly.

To Reconsider
Definition and Purpose

To Reconsider is to call back for further consideration by the assembly an action previously taken on a main motion. Its purpose is to permit a vote taken on a main motion *in the same meeting, session, or convention* to be set aside, and the motion again considered and voted on as if no previous vote had been taken on it.

Requirements (D,M)

To Reconsider is debatable (D), not amendable, and requires a majority vote (M) to pass. It may be withdrawn. It may not be moved on the same motion twice, and a vote on the motion To Reconsider may not itself be reconsidered. Its consideration may not be referred to a committee or postponed, but motions To Limit (Extend the Limits of) Debate, To Close Debate, and To Withdraw may be applied to it. The motion To Reconsider may be made while another main motion is pending, but its consideration is delayed until there is no other main motion pending. It may be applied only to votes on main motions, since other motions that have failed may be renewed after intervening business, and other motions that have passed may be changed by other procedural motions. For example, a passed motion To Refer may be changed by recalling from the committee the referred motion, and a passed motion To Postpone may be changed by a motion to resume consideration of the postponed motion.

Forms and Examples

1. Member: Mr. Chairperson, I move To Reconsider the vote on the motion that we contribute $100 toward the political campaign of Governor Wilson.

	Chair:	A motion To Reconsider the vote on the motion that we contribute $100 toward the campaign of Governor Wilson is before you for discussion. Since no part of the $100 has been contributed and no other official action has been taken under the motion, the vote on the motion may be reconsidered. The floor is open for discussion on the motion.
2.	Member:	Ms. President, I move To Reconsider the vote on the motion that we attend church this Sunday as a group.
	Chair:	A motion To Reconsider the vote on the motion that we attend church this Sunday as a group is before you for consideration. [Discussion] Those in favor of reconsidering the vote on the motion that we attend church this Sunday as a group, please say Aye. Those opposed, please say No. [Vote.] The motion To Reconsider has passed and the motion that we attend church this Sunday as a group is again before us, just as it was before we voted on it. Is there discussion?
		or
		The motion To Reconsider has not passed. We shall continue with the next item on the agenda.
3.	Member:	Mr. Chairman, I move To Reconsider the vote on the motion that we hire an architect to plan the enlargement of our clubhouse.
	Chair:	It is noted that a motion To Reconsider the vote on [stating the

motion] has been made. We shall return to this motion To Reconsider following the disposition of the main motion now before us. Let us continue with our discussion of the main motion.

Discussion   This infrequently used motion permits an assembly to reexamine an action taken earlier that it subsequently finds questionable. It is in order only during the meeting, session, or convention in which the vote to be reconsidered was taken. Unwise actions discovered after a meeting closes, may usually be corrected by the motion To Rescind, discussed in the next section.

The motion To Reconsider may be made by any member,[1] and may be applied to affirmative or negative votes on main motions, but not to votes on motions that may be renewed within a reasonable time, such as To Amend, To Refer, and To Postpone, or to votes which have already resulted in irreversible action.

If the meeting, session, or convention is adjourned—not just recessed—before the motion To Reconsider is taken up, it is as if the motion had never been presented. If made when nothing else is pending, the motion To Reconsider is handled immediately.

An alert presiding officer should not permit abuse of the motion To Reconsider. A motion to reconsider a vote immediately after the vote is

---

[1]Luther S. Cushing (*Manual of Parliamentary Practice* [Philadelphia: David McKay Company, 1925], p. 208) does not require that reconsideration be moved by a member who "voted on the prevailing side" of the motion in question. Henry M. Robert (*Robert's Rules of Order Newly Revised* [Glenview, Ill.: Scott, Foresman and Company, 1970], p. 265, Joseph F. O'Brien (*Parliamentary Law for the Layman* [New York: Harper and Brothers, 1952], p. 143), and George Demeter (*Demeter's Manual of Parliamentary Law and Procedure* [Boston: Little, Brown, and Company, 1969], p. 156), among others, make this stipulation. Alice Sturgis (*Sturgis Standard Code of Parliamentary Procedure*, 2nd ed. [New York: McGraw-Hill, 1966], p. 41) points out the inappropriateness of this requirement.

taken, intended to prevent a later motion To Reconsider (since a vote may not be reconsidered a second time), should not be tolerated; nor should its use *ad nauseam* by a disgruntled minority to waste time and heckle the majority.

To Reconsider permits an assembly to correct an action taken under a misapprehension or with inadequate information. The vote on any main motion, whether passed or lost, may be reconsidered at the same meeting, session, or convention in which it was acted on. No vote on a main motion may be reconsidered, however, if some irreversible action has been taken on it, such as a payment of money, signing of a contract, or notification of an appointment and acceptance by the party concerned.

Summary

To Rescind
Definition and Purpose

To Rescind is to nullify a decision or action that cannot be changed by the motion To Reconsider. Its purpose is to cancel, or make void, the results of a motion previously passed.

Requirements (D,A,M)

To Rescind is a main motion, in order only when no other main motion is pending. It is debatable (D), may be amended (A), *only* as to the portion of the decision to be rescinded, and requires a majority vote (M) to pass. It may be applied to main motions and to votes on appeals from the decision of the presiding officer. To Rescind opens to debate the main motion that it is intended to nullify. To Rescind may have applied to it the motions To Amend, To Refer, To Postpone, To Limit (Extend the Limits of) Debate, To Close Debate, and To Withdraw.

Forms and Examples

1. Member: Ms. Chairperson, I move To Rescind the decision taken at our last meeting that our convention be held in Boston.
    Chair: A motion To Rescind the decision taken in the last meeting

that our convention be held in Boston is before you for discussion.

If passed, the chair states:

The motion To Rescind the decision taken in the last meeting that our convention be held in Boston has passed. Therefore, that action no longer stands. The next item on the agenda is . . .

2. Member: Mr. President, I move To Rescind the motion passed last fall that this faculty award an honorary doctorate of laws to Mr. Marshall at our June graduation.

Chair: The motion To Rescind the action of last fall awarding an honorary degree to Mr. Marshall is before you for discussion.

Member: Mr. President, I question entertaining the motion To Rescind this motion since certain actions have been taken that may not be undone.

Chair: Please explain your position.

Member: Extensive publicity has already been given the faculty decision, and the proposed recipient of the degree has been notified of the action and agreed to be present to receive it. Therefore, I believe it is not possible To Rescind and the motion is out of order.

Chair: The chair stands corrected. The member is right, and the motion To Rescind is out of order.

Discussion   It makes no difference how long ago the main motion to be rescinded was passed. Motions may not be rescinded, however, if irreversible actions have already been taken on them. For example, if money has already been paid for legal services, the action authorizing payment may not be rescinded. Or, if a person has been elected to membership, been officially notified, and accepted, the action may not be rescinded. However, unexecuted portions of a motion may be rescinded.

If a passed motion is rescinded, the minutes should record the passage of a motion To Rescind and also a statement of the motion, or the portion of a motion, rescinded.

To prevent fluctuations in attendance from permitting a smaller group to reverse a decision of a larger group, advance notice of the motion To Rescind may be required for a majority vote to pass; a two-thirds vote may be required to pass if no advance notice is given. Such a requirement may be adopted as a rule of order; but in the absence of such stipulations, a majority vote prevails. The vote required To Rescind, however, should never be lower than the vote that was necessary to pass the motion in question. That is, a two-thirds vote is necessary To Rescind a motion that required a two-thirds vote to pass.

Summary

The motion To Rescind, although seldom used, permits an assembly to rectify mistakes made in haste, to take into account new developments, or to invalidate motions passed by an unrepresentative minority in a poorly attended meeting. Any main motion or portion of a motion, passed by an assembly may be rescinded, provided that irreversible action has not been taken on it.

Motions Not Recommended

6

Motions Not
Recommended

The thesis of this work is that parliamentary procedure may be simplified, and still make all the necessary provisions for an organization to conduct its business. This is accomplished by eliminating several motions, still included in most other manuals, which almost invariably result in confusion. The functions served by these motions are either considered unnecessary or are fulfilled by other ordinary or special motions that are more easily used and understood.

Some of these motions have nonsensical names, such as To Lay on the Table, To Postpone Indefinitely, or The Previous Question. Others are so complicated that few members of groups feel competent to invoke them, such as To Object to the Consideration and To Reconsider and Have It entered on the Minutes. Some are so infrequently used that they have never been heard in thousands of organizations, such as To Fix the Time to Which to Adjourn, To Make a General or a Special Order, To Call for the Orders of the Day, To Refer to a Committee of the Whole, and To Expunge from the Record. Others are used—and sometimes overused—when simpler and clearer methods for accomplishing the same purposes exist, such as To Raise a Question of Privilege, To Rise to a Parliamentary Inquiry, To Amend the Amendment, and To Close Nominations. Explanations of the decisions to eliminate these motions and to simplify procedure generally, will be found in the following discussions of individual motions.

To Postpone Indefinitely

To Postpone Indefinitely, a motion whose name contradicts itself, is to reject a main motion without requiring members to vote on it directly. Two purposes of the motion are to take a *straw vote* to determine the strength of the opposing side, and to dispose of a motion undeserving of consideration without recording a vote on the motion itself. Small wonder that many have advocated dropping To Postpone Indefinitely! Complicated rules of gamesmenship are not needed in serious group deliberations.

The motion To Withdraw is available to get rid of unsatisfactory motions. It may be offered at any time and means just what it says, in both of its principal forms: when invoked by the original mover of a motion, it is a Request to Withdraw, usually granted routinely by general consent; when offered by a member other than the mover of the motion to be withdrawn, it is a motion That [stating the motion] be Withdrawn, and maybe passed by general consent, or by majority vote. As a way of removing a motion from consideration, To Withdraw eliminates the confusion built into using To Postpone Indefinitely.

To Amend the Amendment

To Amend the Amendment may not trouble students of parliamentary procedure, but it has long been a source of confusion and frustration for those who have not made a special study of procedural rules. The terminology is inherently confusing. Skillful and experienced presiding officers are hard-pressed to state clearly the parliamentary situation when more than one proposed amendment is pending. Only one amendment, the last one stated by the presiding officer, is immediately pending but it is unlikely that all members understand why *three votes* are required to approve a main motion, a motion To Amend, and a motion To Amend the Amendment.

The function served by the motion To Amend the Amendment must be preserved, while its ambiguity and the difficulty of stating and handling the motion are simplified. There is no need to use the term To Amend the Amendment. Changes in a proposed amendment may be accepted informally, as they usually are in small groups, or by general consent. If there is an objection to accepting a change in a proposed amendment, a vote may be taken on the proposed amendment with the understanding that the suggested change may subsequently be proposed as a separate amendment. This procedure is discussed more fully under To Amend in Chapter 4.

The artificiality of a group referring the consideration of a motion to itself, under the pretense that functioning as a single large committee will allow it to proceed more effectively in its deliberations, approaches the ridiculous. And when the group later moves To Rise and Report to itself, in order to shed its playacting role as a committee and resume normal status, the ludicrousness of the situation is undeniable. Perhaps that is why these motions are never used in most organizations. A group may vote to allow itself any degree of informality in procedure, including a recess for the utmost freedom in consideration, without resorting to the subterfuge of these motions.	To Refer to a Committee of the Whole, To Consider as if in a Committee of the Whole

Two good reasons for dropping this motion are that it does not mean what it says and that its intended use has been generally abused. The consideration of a motion is never literally laid on the table, or tabled. In the interest of accuracy and simplification, the names of motions should reveal their purposes. The purpose of this motion—to put aside temporarily the consideration of a motion—is well served by the motions To Postpone or To Recess.	To Lay on the Table, To Table

To Table is now generally used, in the Congress of the United States and elsewhere, to kill a motion—another instance of the misleading use of language. Because the motion is undebatable, members may vote on it without ever learning why the mover wants the consideration tabled, unless reasons are stated in his motion To Table. Perhaps that is why many members often abstain from voting on a motion To Table, and a relatively small group of organized opponents of a motion may constitute the majority voting To Table or kill it.

If one's intent is to kill a motion, the motion To Withdraw should be used and the reasons for withdrawal explained openly and honestly; if the intent is to postpone consideration, the motion of that name is self-explanatory. Both motions have the virtue of permitting debate on the wisdom of taking such action.

The Previous Question

The Previous Question is currently used to close debate when further deliberation is no longer profitable or desirable. This function is served by the motion To Close Debate, whose name means just what it says. Therefore, To Move the Previous Question, or To Call for the Previous Question, both incongruent expressions that usually require translation, should be eliminated. Their continued use cannot be defended on any ground other than loyalty to historical precedent.

To Fix the Time to Which to Adjourn

There is no need for this awkwardly stated motion which is almost never used outside of instructional meetings in parliamentary procedure. A motion To Adjourn is debatable and amendable as a main motion if its effect would be to adjourn without providing for another meeting—that is, to disband the organization. If it is necessary to set a time for the next meeting, the motion To Recess until [stating the date and time] meets this need.

To Raise Question of Privilege, To Rise to a Parliamentary Inquiry

These are not motions, but procedures for making an individual request for action or information on procedure. These stereotyped forms are not needed to accomplish the purposes intended. In urgent situations involving the safety or comfort of members, any member should be privileged to ask the presiding officer to effect a remedy immediately, without having to resort to these forms. The degree of urgency should determine whether a speaker may be interrupted; if the presiding officer believes immediate action is required, he may even recess the assembly.

Many organizations do not differentiate between these two procedures and the Point of Order, considering all individual inquiries as Points of Order. Though this is not the use originally intended for a Point of Order, it is less confusing to allow a Point of Order to subsume these forms, since in all such cases the presiding officer decides on the validity of the request.

The Point of Order is the most logical refuge for these two obsolete forms (as well as for To Rise to a Point of Personal Privilege and To Request Leave to Ask a Question) since it allows members to appeal the decision of the chair, as discussed in Chapter 5. Use of the Point of Order to include all these functions is recommended with the understanding that the presiding officer must control the use of a Point of Order, subject to appeal by the assembly.

To Object to the Consideration

This is another unnecessarily complicated motion that cannot be put to a vote in the same language in which it is presented. Members and presiding officers of organizations cannot be blamed for steering clear of a motion that is not debatable, not amendable, requires a "two-thirds negative vote to sustain the objection," and is in order only immediately after the motion to which it applies has been stated by the chair.

If a reason for objecting to the consideration becomes apparent during the discussion of a motion, it is too late to object to its consideration; but it is not too late, of course, to request that it be withdrawn. The principal purpose of the motion is to prevent irrelevant, frivolous, or embarrassing motions from being considered.

These the presiding officer should rule out of order anyway, either on his own initiative or by an affirmative ruling on a Point of Order requesting that the proposed motion be ruled out of order. If the ruling of the chair is reversed by an appeal, the motion must be considered. This procedure bypasses the awkward two-thirds negative vote to sustain the objection, and permits a majority vote—the vote appealing the chair's decision—to decide what may or may not be considered.

Mason[1] allows the Objection to the Consideration, though infrequently used, to be decided by a majority vote in legislative groups. Sturgis[2] follows Robert in requiring a two-thirds vote, on the grounds that every member has a right to have his motion considered. But Sturgis and Robert provide for the presiding officer either to initiate the Objection to the Consideration and put it to a vote, requiring a two-thirds negative vote to prevent consideration; or to rule the motion out of order. If an appeal follows that is lost by majority vote, the ruling of the chair is reversed and the question is considered. In the first instance, a two-thirds negative vote is required to prevent consideration; in the second instance, a majority vote in the negative overrides the presiding officer's decision to rule the motion out of order and thus assures consideration.

It scarcely seems necessary to require a two-thirds vote to prevent consideration of a motion that, if considered, would be decided by a majority vote. The basic principle of majority rule should be sufficient protection of the right of members to present motions for consideration. Furthermore, since the presiding officer should rule out of order all motions he deems frivolous and unnecessary, the question of consideration is decided by a majority vote if his ruling that the motion is out of order is appealed.

[1]Paul Mason, *Manual of Legislative Procedure* (New York: McGraw-Hill Book Company, 1953), p. 222.
[2]Alice Sturgis, *Sturgis Standard Code of Parliamentary Procedure*, 2nd ed. (New York: McGraw-Hill, 1966), p. 90

If the presiding officer is in doubt whether a motion is in order, he should proceed as he does when he wishes the assembly to decide whether a proposed amendment is germane. That is, he should say, "The chair is in doubt as to whether or not the proposed amendment is in order. Those in favor of considering the amendment. . . ." If a majority favors consideration, it is as if the presiding officer had ruled the amendment out of order, and had his ruling appealed and reversed by a majority vote in the negative.

In the interest of simplification of the rules, the Objection to the Consideration should be eliminated. Its continued use is not recommended. If during the debate on a motion, legitimate reasons become apparent to question the propriety of a motion under consideration, a motion To Withdraw is in order. This procedure gives all members, including the presiding officer, more leeway to question the wisdom of considering a motion.

Robert's Rules of Order Newly Revised[3] devotes seven pages to discussing how questions become General Orders and Special Orders, and the complicated procedure for determining the priority or rank of these orders in the meeting to which they are assigned. Robert assumes that an organization's order of business will include the heading Orders of the Day, which designates questions whose consideration has been postponed to a certain day or hour. If a question is made a Special Order, which requires a two-thirds vote, all other business is suspended at the time designated to consider it.

This is an unnecessary procedure for voluntary organizations or for those that meet only annually. The secretary and other officers of such

To Make a General or a Special Order

---

[3]Henry M. Robert, *Roberts Rules of Order Newly Revised* (Glenview, Ill.: Scott, Foresman and Company, 1970), pp. 309–315.

organizations can be trusted to see that items postponed until a particular meeting are on the agenda of that meeting, and are considered, without resorting to General Orders and Special Orders.

To Call for the Orders of the Day

To Call for the Orders of the Day is to remind the presiding Officer to redirect the assembly's attention to the agenda from which it has wandered. Though customarily used in this way, its technical purpose is to remind the presiding officer that the time has arrived to consider a matter previously postponed. Since it is recommended that General and Special Orders be eliminated, To Call for the Orders of the Day is of little value.

A reminder to the presiding officer to adhere to the agenda is best accomplished by a request that needs no further translation, such as, "Madam Chairwoman, I believe we omitted the report of the treasurer."[4] If stronger measures are necessary to get the floor, a member may rise to a Point of Order to remind the presiding officer of the need to return to the agenda.

To Close Nominations

This motion is unnecessary. When it is in order, it is superfluous, since nominations have for all practical purposes already been closed; otherwise, it is premature and hence out of order. Robert states that a chairman should not entertain the motion until after a reasonable time has been allowed for nominations to be presented, and Sturgis goes as far as to state that a motion To

[4]As recommended by Robert W. English in "Motions which Should be Abolished" *Parliamentary Journal* 5 (July, 1964): 30–31. English includes among motions that should be abolished all those included in this chapter except To Amend the Amendment, To Close Nominations, and To Make a General or Special Order.

Close Nominations is not required.[5] It should never be used to deprive a member of his right to nominate the candidate of his choice.

The motion To Close Nominations serves as a routine signal that the election may now proceed. The alert presiding officer will not need to rely on the motion To Close Nominations, but at the appropriate time will say, "If there are no further nominations [pausing], we will proceed with voting on the nominees for the office of vice president. Will the tellers please distribute the ballots?"

To Reconsider and Have It Entered on the Minutes

This is another motion with an esoteric and questionable purpose; to permit a minority that regards itself as disadvantaged because absentee members prevent it from being a majority to render meaningless a decision by the majority. To be eligible to move To Reconsider the Vote on [stating the motion] and Have It Entered on the Minutes, according to Robert,[6] a member must have voted on the prevailing side of the motion whose vote is to be reconsidered; thus, recognizing certain defeat, a member may change his vote from the minority to the majority to establish his eligibility to move To Reconsider and Have It Entered on the Minutes.

The effect of the motion To Reconsider and Have It Entered on the Minutes, if passed, is to prevent any action being taken on the decision in question until the vote on it is reconsidered at the next meeting. It is difficult to understand how a motion whose purpose is to prevent the rule of the majority from prevailing can be defended. Its use permits the minority to determine what constitutes valid action on the part of the majority.

[5]*Robert's Rules*, p. 242; *Sturgis Standard Code*, p. 148.

[6]*Robert's Rules*, p. 265. Sturgis, among other authorities, no longer recognizes this procedure as having any validity; *Sturgis Standard Code*, p. 41.

This contradicts a basic principle of parliamentary law, that of majority rule.

To Expunge from the Record

This motion, if passed, requires the secretary to write across the section of the minutes in question the words "Expunged by action of [date]." The record itself is not erased. Since the action in question may be nullified by the motion To Rescind, the strong feeling implied in expunging from the record has little justification.

To Call for a Division of the Assembly

The purpose of this request is to check on the accuracy of an announced vote. A method of accomplishing this purpose must, of course, be retained, but the expression is archaic. Assemblies do not divide even when they are requested to. Instead, the presiding officer simply calls for another vote, using a method that provides for a more accurate count, such as a show of hands, a rising vote, or ballots. Thus, the purpose of this motion can be effected by a request that the vote be taken again, by another method, stated in clear language that requires no further explanation.

To Dispense with the Reading of the Minutes

The problem with this motion is to determine what it means. "To dispense with" usually means to do without, but the motion as commonly invoked makes no provision for the *approval* of the minutes. In its present form it is ambiguous and should be abandoned. Other more specifically worded motions may be substituted to fulfill related purposes such as: To omit reading of the minutes and approve them as printed in the call for this meeting; To Refer the minutes for approval to the Executive Committee; To Postpone reading of the minutes and have them printed and distributed to the members for consideration at the next meeting; To Refer the consideration of the minutes to the Organization and Rules Committee, which shall be authorized to approve the minutes or to make any changes necessary for accuracy.

Conducting the Meeting

7

Conducting the Meeting

Most authorities agree that the presiding officer should remain impartial. He certainly should be so while administering parliamentary rules. But may he participate in the debate on a motion under consideration, and still be an impartial presiding officer? Many presiding officers openly offer "some remarks on the motion" while still in the chair, thoroughly shattering the image of impartiality, at least on the question under consideration.

While practically every presiding officer will, on occasion, reveal his partiality, either indirectly by his attitude or directly by his comments, to do so reduces his effectiveness as a presiding officer. If he wishes to speak for or against the adoption of a motion, the presiding officer owes it to the membership to step down at least to the same physical and psychological level as other members when he participates in debate. He does this simply by requesting a vice president or another officer of the organization to "take the chair" during the discussion and vote on the motion under consideration. He resumes the chair routinely after the vote has been announced on the motion under consideration. This is a time-honored procedure, and a presiding officer of integrity who perceives his role accurately will recognize his obligation to relinquish the chair when he wishes to add his voice to the discussion on a motion.

Duty to Preside The procedural difficulties encountered by groups in decision making tend to vary inversely with the presiding officer's knowledge and skill in parliamentary procedure. This holds true, of course, only if the presiding officer evaluates his role as serving the group, striving for fair play among members, trying honestly to ascertain the intent of individuals and of the group as a whole, and providing guidance for the fulfillment of this intent. The effective presiding officer never forgets that he is the servant of the assembly, presiding at their pleasure, and the guardian of the assembly's rules of procedure, not his own.

The presiding officer must know the basic principles and essential rules of parliamentary procedure. His knowledge may be rudimentary, lacking the ready facility acquired only through practice, but he cannot be excused from knowing the fundamentals required to present , modify, refer, and postpone motions, and to bring them to a vote in an orderly and efficient fashion.

Knowledge of how to conduct a meeting is, unfortunately, rarely a qualification for election to office. If this lack of knowledge continues, a wise competent leader risks exposing himself to embarrassment, and even ridicule. In cases of extreme inability to conduct a meeting, the presiding officer may rely heavily on the parliamentarian, even to the extent of having him preside temporarily.[1]

It is important that the presiding officer refuse to get "rattled or confused about what is going on in the meeting. Any presiding officer who permits members to speak at will, to offer main motions when a main motion is already under consideration, to interrupt speakers, or to claim the floor without the recognition of the chair is failing in his role as leader. The effective presiding officer refuses to be interrupted after a motion has been proposed until he has either ruled the

[1]See Ray E. Keesey, "Don't Ask the Parliamentarian," *Delaware School Journal* (March, 1959): 12, 14. Reprinted in *Today's Speech* 8 (November, 1960): 15. J. Jeffery Auer says much the same thing in his *Essentials of Parliamentary Procedure*, 3rd ed. (New York: Appleton-Century-Crofts, 1959), p. 47.

motion out of order or stated the motion and placed it before the assembly for discussion. To do otherwise is to invite turmoil.

An effective presiding officer, equally sensitive to his role as judge of acceptable procedure and to the emotional ramifications of judgment, never rules a member out of order as if delighted in his own authority and knowledge of the rules. No member deserves such harsh treatment.

Whenever the presiding officer rules a motion out of order, he should explain why it is out of order, and advise the mover when it would be in order, or how the mover's intent, if known, might be accomplished by the use of another procedure. The presiding officer might also assure the member that he will return to him later, when his motion is in order.

Unlimited patience and a concern for fair play, attributes said to have been possessed in good measure by Henry M. Robert himself, are invaluable when presiding over meetings. Mrs. Henry M. Robert, Sr. relates the story of a man who traveled from Chicago to Milwaukee just to observe Robert presiding over a meeting. He evidently had been hoping for a grandiose performance, and returned to Chicago in disgust, saying, "Nothing happened—everything went like clockwork!"[2] No finer compliment could be paid to any presiding officer.

One cannot overemphasize that the presiding officer's attitude of objectivity and humanity must be genuine, and perceived as such by the assembly, if he is to be successful. In a very real sense, the way the presiding officer interprets his role will determine the "climate" of the group's deliberations.

Organizations should adopt, and include in their *rules of order*, a systematic plan for considering items in meetings. Such a plan is traditionally

The Order of Business

[2]See Joseph F. O'Brien, "Henry M. Robert as Presiding Officer," *"Quarterly Journal of Speech"* 42 (April, 1956): 157–62.

referred to as the *order of business*, agenda, calendar, or program. An organization is, of course, free to adopt any plan appropriate to its purpose and needs, but in the absence of special needs, the following plan may prove convenient:

Order of Business for
a Session of an Assembly

1. Presentation of minutes
2. Reports of officers, boards, and standing committees
3. Reports of special committees
4. Unfinished business
5. New business

Such an order of business provides the needed structure for a meeting and serves to notify members when certain items may be expected to come up for consideration. Changing the order of business, when desired, is possible by general consent or by a two-thirds vote "To Suspend the Rules. This procedure is outlined in the section on suspending the rules in Chapter 5.

Recognition of Speakers The presiding officer must be fair in recognizing speakers in debate. There is nothing wrong with the time-honored custom of awarding the floor first to the mover of the motion in question or to the member to whom he relinquishes this privilege. This is a bit of parliamentary courtesy that is appreciated, and deserved.

As a rule, the presiding officer should allow for the alternation of speakers pro and con motions under consideration. He should recognize, however, that some members who deserve a hearing are neither pro or con. Those who have needed technical information should testify as experts. Others may wish to present a compromise or an amendment to salvage the desirable aspects of a motion and discard the undesirable ones. Therefore, the presiding officer cannot always proceed as if there were only two sides to an issue.

He should guard against recognizing "big shots" to the exclusion of not-so-well-known members who wish to share in the discussion. And he should be ready to refuse firmly to recognize members who claim the floor a second or third time before others have had their first turn to speak. Members will respect a presiding officer who is scrupulously fair in administering parliamentary rules even if, on occasion, some of them feel piqued; but they will be quick to blame the presiding officer who shows partisanship in awarding the floor.

It sometimes becomes necessary for the presiding officer to assume leadership in keeping order in the assembly. If a nonmember is at the center of a disturbance, the presiding officer may invite him, after appropriate warning, to leave the meeting; this action is a ruling from the chair, and may be appealed by a member, but not by the nonmember. Disturbances may be in the nature of continued interruption of speakers, heckling, slander, profane language and the like. An organization has the authority to control its own meeting and to determine who, if anyone, may be present other than its own members.

Disciplinary Measures

It is imperative that the presiding officer remain calm in such circumstances and in no case indulge in shouting or frantic gavel-hammering to quiet a disturber. If the occasion requires it, the presiding officer may state his willingness to entertain a motion to exclude all nonmembers from the meeting—sometimes called a motion To Go into Executive Session. This is a nondebatable motion that may not be amended and requires a majority vote to pass.

Disturbances by members may also require the presiding officer to take action. Particularly obstreperous members may be requested by the presiding officer to make less noise. Members who demand the floor after exhausting their rights to debate or, worse, continue to talk without having been recognized by the chair must be dealt with. A warning from the presiding officer should suffice. A second unheeded warning should alert the presiding officer that more drastic action is needed, and he may direct the member to be seated. If necessary, the presiding officer may invite a motion to censure the offending member, explaining that this becomes a matter of record in the minutes of the organization. If offered, the motion is debatable and should require a two-thirds vote to pass. Likewise, a motion to exclude a member from the meeting is debatable and requires a two-thirds vote. The offending member should be permitted to speak in his own defense, and the secretary may be called on to read examples of offensive remarks that he was directed to record during the proceedings.

Members excluded from a meeting by vote of the assembly, but who refuse to leave, invite more serious action by the assembly. The presiding officer may appoint other members to escort the offending member from the meeting, or the local police may be called to remove him. The organization should be prepared to press formal charges if such extreme action is necessary. If it is anticipated that serious trouble may occur in a meeting, it is probably wise to alert the police and to request the presence of policemen.

The presiding officer himself has no authority to discipline members, but he may conduct the procedures for disciplining members at the direction of the assembly. In fact, the presiding officer may himself be disciplined or removed from office, a procedure explained in Chapter 20 of *Robert's Rules*, which also outlines methods for formally charging members with offenses, preparing defenses, and conducting trials.

Voting Procedures   As a member of the group, the presiding officer has the same right to vote as any other member. Unless he especially wants his vote recorded, however, it is probably wise for the presiding officer to vote only in cases in which his vote would change the outcome. Thus he may vote to break or create a tie, and to prevent or make possible a two-thirds vote. He should always participate when the vote is by secret ballot, whether or not he wishes to write anything on the ballot.

The conventional procedures for handling motions should be carefully followed by the presiding officer, largely to insure that all members understand what is under consideration and what is being voted on. Assuming an uncomplicated motion such as "that we give ten dollars to the Red Cross" has been made by a member, the presiding officer should follow these steps:

1. The presiding officer states the motion and invites discussion.

    Chair: The motion that we give ten dollars to the Red Cross is now before you. Is there any discussion?

2. Discussion ended, the presiding officer restates the motion in its final form and asks for the affirmative vote followed by the negative vote. That order is never reversed.

    Chair: If there is no further discussion, we are now voting on the motion that we give ten dollars to the Red Cross. Those in favor of the motion, please say "aye." Those opposed say "no." (If preferred, the words "yes" and "no" may be used.)

3. The presiding officer announces the result of the voting and adds any necessary information to interpret or to effect the decision.

    Chair: The motion is carried, and the treasurer will present our check

for ten dollars to the local Red
Cross.

or

The motion is lost [or defeat-
ed] and we have decided against
the motion that would have us
give ten dollars to the Red Cross.
The next item on our agenda
is . . .

All of these steps are essential for clarity. Since
considerable time may elapse between Steps 1 and
2, and changes may be made to the motion as
presented in Step 1, it is imperative that Step 2
be followed to the letter. Omission or abridge-
ment of Step 2 has caused many a member to
murmur, "Hey, just what are we voting on?" or
to abstain from voting out of confusion.

Chairman by Decree

If the presiding officer is not elected by the assembly but appointed, as in the case of some chair-
men of boards of corporations, university presidents, and college deans, he is known as a *chairman by decree*.[3] To expect impartiality of a chairman by decree is unrealistic; he is serving two
masters, and his first loyalty is probably to the
authority to whom he owes his position. What
may be expected in such cases is precise definition
of the assembly's legitimate areas of jurisdiction,
and an agreed-upon division of responsibilities,
so that the presiding officer is not put in the pre-
carious position of presiding over the consideration of motions that threaten his relationship with
his superiors or his very position. We delude our-
selves if we expect impartiality under these circumstances.

[3]See Ray E. Keesey, "Chairman by Decree," *Parliamentary Journal* 10 (July, 1969): 3–6 for a further discussion of the anomal-
ous situation of a chairman who was not elected by the assembly he presides over. William S. Tacey, in "Chairman by
Decree Ousted," *Parliamentary Journal* 10 (October, 1969): 20–23
suggests meeting this situation in college faculties by allowing
the faculty to elect its own presiding officer.

When the presiding officer of a group is a power figure, perhaps one to whom the rank-and-file members owe their positions, current status, and salary increments, they are forced to settle for something less than normal freedom in decision making. Such a group is not democratic because of the inequality of membership. The bylaws of such an organization should protect both the presiding officer and the membership by spelling out in detail the authority granted the presiding officer that does not stem from the membership. And the members have a right to know, and to have stated in the bylaws, the limitations under which they must operate. It is well to remember that a meeting conducted by a chairman by decree is equally difficult for both parties, the presiding officer and the members.

Participating Members

The members of an organization who participate actively in its deliberations will find their contributions considerably enhanced if they are familiar with basic procedure. With a simplified procedure, it is not too much to expect that members be familiar with the ordinary motions used to amend, refer, and postpone; to limit and close debate; and to recess and adjourn. These procedures are more than will be required in most meetings.

In addition to knowing parliamentary procedure, members are expected to exhibit just and orderly behavior. Members will abide by decisions of the chair (unless an appeal is in order), refrain from discrediting individuals when they should be attacking arguments, exercise courtesy toward others, be restrained in language and action, and cheerfully (on the surface, at least) work to implement a majority decision even if they voted with the minority.

The Secretary

The *secretary* keeps the official record. He should be seated close to the presiding officer, and observe carefully all that occurs as he takes notes, later to be rewritten in the form desired by the organization. He is the presiding officer's "right hand," providing him with a copy of the agenda; the minutes of the previous meeting; committee reports if available; and a list of unfinished business. He brings to the meeting materials that may be needed, such as the minute book of the organization, up-to-date copies of the bylaws, and a quantity of ballots.

The secretary should know the previous legislative record of the organization, and should serve as a source of information for the presiding officer and members when questions arise about actions previously taken. He keeps an official roster of the membership with him in the meeting. He should be familiar with parliamentary procedure and be able, on occasion, to preside in the absence of the usual presiding officer.

The *minutes* of an organization include a record of all official actions taken, the presiding officer, the presence of a quorum, and information showing that the meeting was duly called and thus legal. The other contents of the minutes will depend upon the degree of detail desired. Some organizations go to the extreme of recording the name of each member who presents a motion, major ideas presented in the discussion, and the numerical count on all votes. Such details are rarely needed and only make the job of the secretary difficult. The exact statement of motions passed should be recorded; the names of participants in the discussion of the motion need not be. It is desirable to include in the minutes the major arguments for and against a motion, but these should not be identified with speakers proposing them since the privilege of discussing a motion freely is jeopardized when what is said becomes a part of public record. Furthermore, it is probably not significant ten years later, what the vote was or who offered the motion. The minutes should be an *official record of actions taken* by the organization, not a transcript of what individuals say in meetings.

Likewise, motions proposed, discussed, and voted down may or may not be entered in the minutes. Complete records must be kept, of course, of all referrals, postponements, and appeals. Amendments need not be entered. If one imagines examining the record ten or twenty years later, a clearer perspective emerges on what is essential. The most common error is to record too much.

If the secretary is a member of the organization, he has the same right to present, discuss, and vote on motions as any other member.

The Parliamentarian

The *parliamentarian*, who advises the presiding officer on parliamentary procedure, should be a specialist, by knowledge and experience. He should be appointed by the presiding officer, not elected. It is probably better if he is not a member of the organization, since he must be an objective and impartial adviser. If he is a member of the organization, he is entitled to his rights —although he cannot exercise them and still remain impartial. He should vote in all secret ballot votes, but in other instances he votes only at risk of losing his image of impartiality. Many organizations, particularly those that hold state, regional, and national conventions, engage a paid professional parliamentarian.[4]

The parliamentarian's work begins prior to the meeting in which he advises the presiding officer. As a condition of accepting an appointment, the parliamentarian should be provided with an up-to-date copy of the bylaws, the program for the meeting in which he is to serve, a copy of the minutes of the previous meeting, and any other information that may help orient him to the organization. The presiding officer and the par-

[4]The American Institute of Parliamentarians maintains a directory of certified professional parliamentarians drawn from its membership. Write to Lester L. Dahms, Executive Director, 3½ West Main Street, Room 211–213, Marshalltown, Iowa 50158.

liamentarian should meet informally before the meeting to discuss parliamentary problems that may arise, determine the extent to which the presiding officer is likely to need help, and brief the parliamentarian on such possible sources of parliamentary intrigue cliques, emotional issues, self-appointed parliamentary strategists, and the like. He may also be available to advise members who request his assistance on motions they wish to present, acceptable procedures, and legitimate strategy to attain desired ends.

The parliamentarian should be easily accessible to the presiding officer during the meeting, preferably seated next to him on the platform. He gives advice on procedure when requested by the presiding officer. It is not unusual for a member to "request a ruling by the parliamentarian" on whether or not a motion is in order, or on some other procedural question. The parliamentarian replies in private to the presiding officer who may, if he wishes, pass on what the parliamentarian has said. The parliamentarian does not answer questions by addressing the assembly, except at the invitation of the presiding officer. He does not make "rulings" even though requested to do so, but he may provide information to assist the presiding officer in making a ruling.

The effective parliamentarian is constantly alert, following closely the progress of the group in handling its agenda. He knows what the immediately pending motion is at all times, and keeps track of motions by using one of the various methods of notetaking for parliamentary proceedings. He must be quick to call the attention of the presiding officer, as unobtrusively as possible, to errors in procedure, and to advise him on correcting the procedure. He must not sit by while serious procedural errors persist, lest there develop a hopeless mess from which the only escape is to disregard pending motions and start over again.

On the other hand, the parliamentarian should not be so fastidious in insisting on letter-perfect procedure that he makes a nuisance of himself. The experienced parliamentarian takes his stand in between the two extremes, and often earns the sincere plaudits of an audience appreciative of his help.

The vice president or vice presidents, the president-elect, the executive secretary, the corresponding secretary, the treasurer, and perhaps the sergeant at arms all occupy positions of significance. Most of these officers, however, do not usually exercise their functions directly in organizational meetings; an exception is the sergeant at arms, and many groups do not have one. Organizations having these officers should spell out in the bylaws their functions, the conditions of their appointment or election, terms of office, procedures for filling vacancies, and the like; it is not necessary to enlarge upon them here.[5]

Other Officials

---

[5]This additional information is available in, among other sources, Alice Sturgis, *Sturgis Standard Code of Parliamentary Procedure*, 2nd ed. (New York: McGraw-Hill, 1966) pp. 160–173.

Committees

8

Committees

Much of the actual work of many organizations is done by committees. It has been said that organizations meet largely to approve what their committees have done. The wisdom of consideration by committee is clear when one recalls that a committee functions with certain inherent advantages over a large assembly. The committee is smaller; operates more informally; is composed of members selected for their competence, knowledge, and willingness to do a particular job; and can go about its work of investigating, holding hearings, and interviewing experts quietly and efficiently. It does the work of the assembly more effectively, and then reports its recommendations.

In spite of all the jokes about committees and some organizations' propensity to form committees at the slightest pretext, the practice of referring considerations to committees is sound. This chapter will look more closely at various kinds of committees, and at some aspects of their functioning.

Standing and Special Committees

Standing committees are provided for in the bylaws of an organization. They remain in existence even though their membership may change with the expiration of terms of office. Most organizations have standing committees for such matters as membership, program, bylaw revision, finance, public relations, and the like.

Special committees are those appointed or elected to do a particular job; they cease to exist when they have reported to the assembly. The members may be appointed by the presiding officer, or elected by the assembly. The size of the committee, the selection process, and the deadline for reporting may all be stipulated in the motion referring consideration to a committee. The person who presides over a special committee may be named by the organization's presiding officer when he appoints the members, may be elected by the committee's members, or may be elected by the assembly. It is common practice for the members of a special committee to be announced by the presiding officer in the meeting in which the committee is authorized—with the first-named member assuming its chair.

Selection of Members The first consideration in assuring a committee's success is wise selection of its members, a factor that may take on increased importance when evaluating the report submitted by the committee. The members should be those most competent and willing to do the task assigned to the committee. If a committee is organized to fulfill a purpose or develop a project already approved by the assembly, its members should obviously be chosen from among those in favor of the proposal.

Other considerations should be kept in mind when selecting committee members. Ordinarily, the committee should be representative of the assembly—that is, its members should represent various interest groups, geographical areas, occupations, and the like. In addition, care should be exercised not to assign a given member to many committees just because he is a willing worker. A committee should normally not be composed entirely of new members of the organization. And its members should be free to devote adequate time to the work of the committee, within the agreed-upon time limits. To prevent a tie vote, most committees should be composed of an odd number of members. The committee should be no larger than necessary, within the limitations imposed by the other considerations mentioned above.

Sometimes the bylaws specify that the organization's president, or another official, shall be an *ex officio* member of all committees or boards; such membership is granted by virtue of office. *Ex officio* membership usually confers all the privileges of other committee members, including the right to vote, but not the obligation to attend meetings regularly. Therefore, unless present, an *ex officio* member should not be counted in determining a quorum.

The presiding officer of a committee needs an understanding of the process of decision making in small groups, as well as special competence in the subject of the committee's work. He needs patience, a willingness to delegate work to others, and an appreciation of the necessity for record-keeping and for writing a report that fairly represents the views of the committee. He may serve as the committee's secretary, as do presiding officers of small committees, or he may appoint a member to serve as secretary. Skill in human relations—the ability to draw out reticent members and prevent more assertive members from dominating the meetings—will stand him in good stead. He needs to recognize the necessity of reminding members of their task when digression threatens to be too time consuming, and, likewise, the beneficial effects of an occasional brief digression in minimizing individual differences that have reached the argumentative stage. While not appearing to hurry deliberations, he gently presses the committee toward its assigned goal.

There is little need for formal parliamentary procedure in committee meetings. The informality typical of a small discussion group is ideal, pro-

Procedure in Committees

vided, of course, that it is not carried to the point of interfering with the committee's progress. The presiding officer sets the tone of the meeting. He should prepare an agenda that includes a statement of the committee's purpose, and should ask for the members' approval of the agenda at the beginning of the meeting. This may not be required in meetings of standing committees, but should not be omitted in special committees.

On occasion, votes must be taken and actions recorded. Usually votes can be taken fairly by general consent at the point when the presiding officer recognizes that the members are in agreement and ready to have that agreement recorded. Unless otherwise stipulated in the bylaws, the quorum for a committee is a majority of its membership.

Informality should prevail in the statement, and possible modifications, of motions. Sometimes a formal statement of a motion is necessary only to reach consensus on how the committee's agreement should be stated in its report. It is a good idea to discuss the wording of a motion informally, instead of following the formal procedure of stating a motion and amending it by vote.

There is usually no time limit on discussion in committee meetings, but its presiding officer should tactfully insure that certain members do not do all the talking. The presiding officer may participate freely in discussion, without restriction on his participation in debate usually found in meetings of the assembly.

The committee's presiding officer should ascertain exactly what has been accomplished in each meeting. Before adjourning, he should seek the committee's approval of the notation he plans to make in the record of its achievements at the meeting. He should include special assignments to committee members to carry on investigations independently, consultants to be interviewed, and special sources to be checked, as well as agreements reached at the meeting and plans for the next meeting. A majority of the committee members present must approve the final report before it may be submitted to the assembly.

The form of a committee's report will vary with its function. A committee appointed to do something, purchase something, conduct an investigation or take action for the assembly will write a report setting forth what was done or purchased, the results of its investigation, or the action taken. For example, a committee appointed to investigate available public address systems and authorized to purchase and have installed in the clubhouse their choice of a new public address system might report as follows:

Committee Reports

Your committee appointed to investigate available public address systems and to purchase the choice recommended by the committee has held two meetings with all members present. The committee has also visited three local audio-electrical appliance companies and had these three submit written bids, drawn to committee specifications, for the public address system. The three bids were reviewed and compared with committee specifications by a special consultant engaged by the committee, whom the committee paid a fee of $50. His recommendation was to purchase the PA system from Dunn Brothers Audio Incorporated, whose bid was $675 after installation. Your committee has agreed to this purchase and the equipment, with a year's guarantee, will be installed on Friday of this week.

Because the committee report summarizes action previously authorized by the assembly, no further action need be taken on the report, except to file it for future reference.

More frequently, however, a committee report includes both a summary of its proceedings and recommendations for proposed action to be taken by the assembly. This occurs when a motion is passed to refer the consideration of a pending main motion to a standing committee or special committee for study and recommendations to guide the assembly.

For example, a city council meeting referred a main motion "that the wattage be doubled in all city lights on Main Street," to a special committee to study and present recommendations. The committee report might take the following form:

Your committee, to which was referred the main motion "that the wattage be doubled in all city lights on Main Street," wishes to report that the committee has met with representatives of the Diamond Electric Company which provides the city with electric power; with the city police committee on crime prevention and control; and with the executive committee of the City Board of Education; and recommends that the motion mentioned be rejected as an oversimplification of the problem. If rejected, the committee will propose a motion to upgrade the city lighting system on a selective basis, increasing the power or lights in areas where crime has increased generally, and will recommend several new installations of lights on city streets. However, the motion to be proposed by the committee is too complicated to arrive at by amending the pending motion and the committee, therefore, recommends the pending motion be defeated.

In its present form, this report need only be filed, perhaps with the thanks of the council for a job well done. The council, with the advice of its committee fresh in mind, would continue consideration of the main motion, perhaps heeding the committee's recommendation to reject it. If so, the council's presiding officer would normally then turn to the presiding officer of the committee and offer him an opportunity to present the new motion his committee promised would be forthcoming if the previous main motion were defeated. Thus the promised recommendation of the committee becomes a main motion, treated like any other main motion and subject to any of the motions (amending, referring, postponing, limiting or closing debate, withdrawing) the council may wish to apply to its consideration.

The report of a committee appointed to set the time, place, and date for an annual meeting, and to suggest broad outlines for the meeting's program should be adopted, not filed, if approved by the assembly; in this case the assembly's adoption is necessary to commit the organization to fulfillment of such actions.

Committee reports may be oral or written, depending upon the degree of formality desired, the difficulty of the subject matter, and the need for written records. A special committee appointed to look into the desirability of holding a group picnic at a certain place and time may present a brief oral report summarizing its findings to the parent group. On the other hand, a committee report on the wisdom of establishing regional conventions, a national headquarters, or a change in basic organizational policy would normally be written and detailed. A written report, especially on important considerations, takes the form of an impersonal communication in the third person addressed to the president and signed by the presiding officer for the committee. It may begin:

Your committee to investigate and recommend with regard to [stating the committee's charge] wishes to report as follows:

A minority report, if submitted, may take a similar form, such as:

The undersigned, not agreeing with the majority of the committee, present a minority report as follows:

To the extent that the committee report is a factual account of the committee's deliberations, expert counsel, hearings, site visitations, subcommittee investigations, and the like, there is no need for a minority report. It is when the committee report enters into the realm of opinion, offering advice to the assembly, that a minority report may be legitimate. Therefore, a minority report will usually include a statement of intent to offer recommendations in the form of main motions that differ from those presented in the committee report. The assembly's approval of the minority report as a substitute for the committee report is understood not to apply to the factual portion of the committee report, only to the recommendations to be presented as main motions for action by the assembly.

In general, formal minority reports are seldom necessary, since any committee member may present to the assembly an opinion that differs from that of the committee. That is, he may propose an amendment to any of the committee's recommendations presented as a main motion for assembly action. He may also announce his intentions to do so during discussion of the committee report. Note that the term *committee report*, not *majority committee report*, is used to refer to the report submitted by a majority of the committee, even if a minority report is filed.

Presentation and Consideration of Reports

Reports from standing committees usually precede those of special committees in the order of business. Standing committees' reports are often presented in the order in which they are listed in the bylaws. The reports of special committees are presented either in the order in which the committees were appointed or in an order determined for each meeting.

The organization's presiding officer usually calls for a committee report by announcing that the report of the (naming the committee) will be presented at this time. Whether or not he names the presiding officer of the committee, it is assumed, unless an announcement is made to the contrary, that the presiding officer of the committee will present the report. The committee's presiding officer should already have provided the secretary with a copy of the committee report.

If the report is long, it should have been duplicated and distributed with the call for the meeting; in this case the presiding officer of the committee may assume that the report has been read, and may ask for discussion without reading it. If the report is routine—consisting of a record of meetings held, topics discussed, and the expected fulfillment of functions assigned, and recommending no action—the committee's presiding officer may simply say, "Our committee's report is printed in the call for the meeting. I will be glad to answer any questions on the report." Following the discussion, if there is any, the presiding officer of the organization should announce, "Since no action is required, the report will be filed."

In order to avoid confusion, it must be clearly stated in the committee's report that its recommendations will be presented in the form of main motions following consideration of the report. The adoption of a committee report which includes recommendations later to be presented as main motions does not commit the assembly to implementing those recommendations. When the committee's recommendations are presented as a main motion, it should not be stated as, "I move adoption of the committee's recommendations that . . .," but, like any other main motion, as "I move that. . . ." This is essential, since the adoption of a committee's recommendation is entirely different than the authorization of an action proposed in the form of a main motion.

Usually, the consideration of a committee report is fairly routine. The report of committee's deliberations may not be amended, except to correct errors of fact; since the assembly may not make the committee say something that it did not say. Of course, clarification may be requested, and the report may be discussed, filed, adopted, rejected, or sent back to the committee for further study, and its consideration may be postponed to a more convenient time.

In the interest of clarity, committee reports should normally be filed, or, if applicable, adopted, but not *received* or *accepted*, since the latter terms are ambiguous and mean different things to different people.

An informational report or progress report should usually not be adopted. To *file* a committee report makes it available to the members for reference, and for reconsideration if necessary, but commits the assembly to nothing. To *adopt* a report commits the assembly to approval of opinions and activities described but does not authorize implementation of its proposed recommendations.

As stated earlier, committee's recommendations are presented as main motions. If a motion is long and controversial, such as a motion to adopt changes in the bylaws presented by a bylaw-revision committee, it may be considered "by paragraph." The term *paragraph* should be taken to refer not to the literary paragraph but to any subdivision of content that may not be further divided; more than one literary paragraph may constitute a subdivision.

The committee's presiding officer reads or—if they have copies of the report—directs the members' attention to "paragraph one," and then pauses while the presiding officer of the organization inquires if there is discussion. The committee may be requested to supply additional information, and an amendment may be proposed, handled like any other proposed amendment, and voted on. Several changes may be authorized this way. When there is no further discussion, the presiding officer directs the committee's presiding officer to proceed with "paragraph two," and so on. A vote is not taken on *the adoption* of paragraph one at this time, although votes on proposed amendments to it may have been taken.

When all the paragraphs have been presented, discussed, and modified to please the assembly, the committee's presiding officer asks for discussion, or further amendments, of *any paragraph in the report*, before the motion "that the changes in the bylaws be adopted" is voted on. The required vote to pass a motion to amend the bylaws would be that stipulated in the bylaws.

Minority reports, which may also be distributed with the call for the meeting, are presented by the spokesman for the minority, who moves that the minority's recommendations be substituted for those in the committee report wherever applicable. This is a proposed amendment to the committee report, and is handled like any other proposed amendment. It should be offered immediately after presentation of the committee report, or immediately after the presiding officer of the committee announces that the committee report is printed in the call for the meeting and is therefore open to discussion. The minority's recommendations, in the form of a substitute amendment, become the immediately pending motion; if passed by a majority vote, they are incorporated into the committee report, replacing the majority's recommendations which are simply filed for reference.

If the spokesmen for the committee report and for the minority report plan to present recommendations as main motions following their reports, it is helpful to have them announce their intention to do so before presenting their reports. They may also indicate informally what these motions will involve, if this information has not already been distributed in printed form.

When an assembly refers the consideration of a motion to a committee—standing or special—the report of the committee should include an accurate statement of the motion referred; the specific charge, if any, to the committee; and the results of the committee's work. A proposed amendment pending when referral was made to the committee is still pending when the committee reports back to the assembly, and the committee may recommend its passage or rejection. The committee may suggest that other changes be made, and may announce its intention to offer amendments after the pending amendment is disposed of. The committee may also propose its own improved version of the referred motion as a substitute amendment. It is important to recognize that the committee report is offered as advice to the assembly, and that even if it is filed or adopted, the assembly still must take official action by voting on the main motion.

Information on Committees in the Bylaws
All standing committees should be named in the constitution or bylaws. (See Chapter 11 for the distinction between the constitution and the bylaws). For each committee, the following information should be provided:

1. Number of members, and number constituting a quorum
2. Special qualifications, if any, for membership
3. Selection process for members
4. Selection process for the presiding officer
5. Terms of office, including provision for "staggering" terms if desired
6. Function
7. Provision for filling vacancies
8. Frequency and time of reports.

The bylaws should also authorize the president or the assembly to create special committees to accomplish particular tasks. The structure of special committees cannot be set forth in the bylaws since it will depend upon the purpose and nature of the committee.

In summary, the presentation and consideration of committees' reports often leads to confusion, much of which could be prevented if organizations spelled out in their bylaws that a committee's recommendations requiring action by the assembly must be presented as separate main motions for consideration and vote by the assembly.

Voting

Voting

When an impatient member of an assembly says, "Let's put it to a vote," referring to the motion under consideration, he is asking the presiding officer to determine the majority vote. A *majority vote* is a majority of eligible votes cast, not counting blanks and abstentions; unless there are special stipulations to the contrary, this is the definition of majority vote that should be applied.

Types of Votes
The Majority Vote

The term has several possible meanings, however, and the bylaws of an organization should stipulate the particular meaning intended if a special definition is applicable. There are at least six different definitions of majority votes:
1. A majority of the eligible votes cast
2. A majority of the members present and voting (same as Number 1)
3. A majority of the members present
4. A majority of the members in good standing
5. A majority of a quorum
6. A majority of the membership. This usually applied to a group with a small fixed membership, such as a State Board of Health, and a prescribed majority, such as a requirement that five of the eight members vote in favor of a motion to carry it, whether or not all members are in attendance.

Decisions may be made by only a small number of the members in attendance. Since members may choose not to vote—that is, to abide by the majority decision—it is possible for a majority vote to represent only a small fraction of the number in attendance. With one hundred members in attendance, the following all represent legal majority votes: 80 to 20, 40 to 10, 20 to 5, 10 to 9, 5 to 3, and 1 to 0.

The Unanimous Vote

Strictly speaking, a *unanimous vote* should mean that all members present and eligible to vote did so, and that all voted the same way. Some liberty is taken with the definition when a presiding officer announces a "unanimous decision" following a vote by general consent. To say that a member did not object is different than saying that he voted.

A more accurate announcement of the results of such a vote would be, "The motion is carried without objection," or "The motion is carried without any dissenting votes." When a member chooses not to vote, and to abide by the decision formed by those who do vote, it is not accurate to announce a decision that suggests he did vote.

It is recommended that the term "by unanimous vote" not be used carelessly. Members may be offended, but not wish to protest its misuse openly. Organizations have been known to pass a motion by majority vote and then, under the impression that it would look better on the record, agree to make the vote unanimous if no one objects. Very little sober reflection is needed to condemn this practice. It offends the basic principle of equality of membership, which guarantees each member the right to vote or to abstain from voting without having to reveal which he did.

The practice of declaring a member who is elected to office by secret ballot as "elected by unanimous vote," if no one objects, fools no one and should likewise be condemned. For the secretary to "cast a unanimous ballot" for a candidate, even if he is unopposed, should never be condoned. A unanimous vote should mean just what it says.

A *two-thirds vote*, used in controlling debate and in votes so stipulated in the bylaws, usually means two-thirds of the eligible votes cast. Other definitions include all the variations listed under the discussion of the majority vote, if one substitutes two-thirds for a majority. In the arithmetic of determining a two-thirds vote, final fractions are given a full vote. For example, two-thirds of fourteen is considered to be ten, as is two-thirds of fifteen; one-third of fourteen is considered to be five, the number necessary to defeat a motion requiring two-thirds if only fourteen votes are cast. For a motion that requires two-thirds vote to pass, there must be twice as many votes in the affirmative as in the negative, or 60 to 30, 10 to 5, 4 to 2, or 2 to 1.

A *plurality* is the highest number of votes received when more than two items or nominees are being voted on, whether or not this number represents a majority of the total votes cast. For example, if 10, 8, and 4 votes are cast for A, B, and C respectively, A has a plurality; no one has a majority (12 votes). If only one issue is under consideration, or if only two candidates are running in an election, the principle of majority rule applies. A plurality vote is not sufficient to pass a motion or to elect a member to office unless the bylaws of the organizations so provide.

In a *tie vote*, the total vote cast is equally divided between the affirmative and the negative, or between two or more candidates. A tie vote is considered a negative vote, not a "deadlock"; it does not pass a motion or elect a candidate to office. If the presiding officer has not already voted, he is eligible to vote. If the tie is not broken, the effect is the same as if the motion had lost by a majority vote in the negative, or, in the case of an election, as if no vote had been taken.

A Two-thirds Vote

The Plurality Vote

The Tie Vote

An exception to the rule that a tie vote is treated as a negative vote occurs when the vote on an appeal from a ruling of the chair results in a tie. Since a majority vote is required to overrule the chair, a tie vote sustains the ruling of the chair.

Changing a Vote

Any member may change his vote before the results are announced, except when the vote is taken by ballot. When the ballots have been collected after voting, it is too late for a vote to be changed.

The Right Not to Vote: Abstaining

It is widely asserted that members have a duty to vote to express their willingness to share in the responsibility of decisions. But no one can be compelled to vote. If he wishes, a member may remain silent in a voice vote, answer "Present" in a roll call vote, or turn in a blank ballot. To abstain from voting, of course, is to help the winning side. Members who do so are bound by the decision of the majority. By not voting, they are, in effect, expressing their willingness to abide by the decision arrived at by the prevailing side.

Sometimes a member will insist that his abstention be officially recorded. He wants the record to show that he did not vote on the motion under consideration. While some people think this is making too much of the privilege of not voting, organizations usually oblige such requests, "if there are no objections," by asking the secretary to record the names of members who abstain from voting. If this practice becomes a problem by delaying unnecessarily the taking of votes, the organization should formulate a policy on recording abstentions and incorporate it into the bylaws.

If a member's personal or financial interest in the outcome of a vote warrants his request that the record show his abstention from voting, the practice is, of course, defensible. On the other hand, any widespread practice of recording abstentions would appear to reflect a misunderstanding of the true meaning of exercising the privilege not to vote.

Methods of Voting
General Consent

Voting by general consent is not the same as voting by unanimous consent, and the presiding officer should not request unanimous votes or unanimous approval on even the most routine matters. In a vote by general consent, the presiding officer declares a motion passed or a request granted "if there is no objection." This is a common procedure and may, in the hands of a skillful presiding officer, be used to expedite the handling of business.

The procedure should be widely used to secure decisions on routine, noncontroversial questions. A presiding officer who is responsive to the generally known wishes of an assembly, and who can accurately detect the "sense of the meeting," may make frequent use of votes by general consent. The method constitutes a legal vote, and motions passed in this way should be recorded by the secretary as official actions.

Misuse of votes by general consent may be, and should be, prevented by any member or members saying, "I object." A single objection forces the presiding officer to take a vote that may be verified by count.

The Voice Vote

Presiding officers vary in the exact words they prefer to put a motion to a vote. Some, after stating the motion to be voted on, announce, "Those in favor of the motion, say Aye. Those opposed, No." Or, "Those in favor, make it manifest by saying Aye. Those voting against the motion, say No." The simplest statement consistent with maximum clarity is the best. A *voice vote* is an oral vote. It is the most frequently used method of voting in organizations of all sizes.

There are limitations, however, to voting by voice when a close vote is anticipated, because of the difficulty of counting the vote. The presiding officer who expects a fairly close vote on a motion saves time in the long run by requesting a vote by show of hands. This will also obviate the problem that arises when a loud minority outshouts a docile majority. The presiding officer should be quick to announce his own confusion in determining the results of such a voice vote, and should request another vote by show of hands. Of course, any member who has reason to question the presiding officer's count of a vote may request that he verify the accuracy of his announcement of a vote.

The Show of Hands   The advantage of voting by a show of hands is accuracy. In groups of up to two hundred people, and sometimes more, the presiding officer may count hands himself, if he has a clear view of the whole assembly. For larger groups it is preferable to appoint tellers to count assigned sections of voters and to report the results to the chief teller or directly to the presiding officer. In large groups in which considerable time is required to count the votes, the presiding officer should probably direct members to "raise your right hand until counted," to alert them against dropping their hands too quickly. The count is accomplished more easily if all members vote by raising their right hands, since the hands are more evenly spaced.

In practice, most votes in large meetings can be quickly and quietly taken by a show of hands, and it is usually a waste of time to count since most votes are overwhelmingly pro or con. Voting by a show of hands helps to maintain decorum in large meetings, since voice votes may be quite noisy. Even a standing vote can usually be taken without counting.

The form varies. Many presiding officers, after stating the motion, announce, "Those in favor, please raise your right hands." After counting (if it appears necessary), he signals for them to drop their hands by saying, "Thank you. [pause] Those opposed, please raise your right hands." And again, after counting, "Thank you." Then the presiding officer announces the result of the vote.

Though seldom necessary, a rising vote is sometimes used to express an emotion, such as gratitude, through "a rising vote of thanks" to someone. It is often used to express respect for a deceased member by voting "to spread on the minutes" a memorial statement outlining his accomplishments and the grief of the organization at his death.

The Rising Vote

In cases of extreme difficulty in determining a vote count by other means, members may be asked to vote by rising, or even to separate into two groups, one affirmative and one negative.

Most people have witnessed dull and time-consuming roll call votes at televised national political conventions. It is a slow method of voting, although often considered the most accurate, and is justified only when it is desirable to make public the members' votes. It is sometimes used as a dilatory tactic by members who hope that the prospect of a roll call vote will cause members to leave, or that some members may balk at publicly recording their votes.

The Roll Call

The ballot is used for voting in elections, and for deciding issues that are emotionally charged and controversial. When it is desirable to conceal one's vote, the ballot may be used. Its use may be ordered on any motion by a majority vote on a nondebatable, nonamendable motion stating the method of voting to be used. Ideally, ballots are

By Ballot

prepared in advance and a member has only to check his preference or preferences. The use of blank ballots is facilitated by writing on a blackboard the names and numbers of the candidates, or other choices, and asking the voter to write the number or numbers of his choice on the ballot.

Tellers collect the ballots and canvass (see page 148) them, counting blanks separately; they then report the results—votes for, against, illegal, and blank—to the presiding officer, who announces the results. Marked but invalid (illegal) votes are counted in the total votes cast to determine a majority; blank votes are ignored in the total count. Many organizations could make wiser use of the ballot method of voting by employing preferential voting, discussed on pages 150–153.

The Mail Vote   A vote by mail may be ordered by a majority vote, provided the bylaws permit this procedure. The bylaws should also specify those responsible for preparing and distributing ballots, the procedure to be followed by the voter in marking and returning his ballot, and those responsible for counting the ballots. It should be remembered that, unless special provisions in the bylaws prevent it, a mail ballot may result in a decision based on a smaller percentage of participation than would be the case if the vote were taken in a regular meeting with a quorum present. One way to control this is for the bylaws to state that decisions by mail are valid only if a majority of a quorum of the members returns ballots.

Voting by mail is frequently used in elections, which may involve the use of a preferential ballot, but may be used for other purposes as well. Organizations may run out of time in their meetings and decide to determine a pending question by a mail ballot rather than by calling additional meetings. Only main motions, not procedural motions growing out of the consideration of main motions, should be voted on by mail.

It should not be possible to order a vote by mail on less than a majority vote. Otherwise, a minority may prevent a majority from taking legitimate action in a meeting. Once a decision has been reached on a motion by a majority vote, it should not be possible to nullify that decision by ordering a vote by mail. Of course, if it later becomes apparent that a mail vote is desirable, the earlier vote may be reconsidered, and a mail vote ordered, if consistent with the bylaws.

A vote by mail is often used by large organizations and corporations whose memberships are widely scattered geographically. Officers are elected, proxies determined (see next section), and propositions submitted for decisions on a ballot mailed to the members with instructions and, often, an envelope.

This cannot be said to be a "secret ballot," although it comes close to being secret if the marked ballot is sealed in an envelope that is signed by the voter, and this envelope is mailed in a second envelope. The ballots themselves are not signed or identified in any way. The tellers compare the signatures on the envelopes against a signed membership roster to determine the legality of ballots submitted. There must be provisions made to verify the legality of votes, and this procedure does so while retaining a reasonable degree of secrecy. A variation is to have the ballots sent, in signed envelopes, to a post office box rented for this purpose and opened on a predetermined date and in the presence of neutral observers. Only one envelope is needed with this method.

Sometimes ballots are distributed in a meeting and, to save time, members are requested to mark, sign, and mail the ballots to the secretary, the chief teller, or someone else designated to receive them. This procedure, sometimes called *open signed ballots*, is no improvement in terms of secrecy upon the method just mentioned, since someone still must verify the authenticity of the ballots.

Brief statements of the positions for and against the motion to be voted on, or a summary of the qualifications of the candidates, may be mailed with the ballots to remind voters of pertinent information.

The Vote by Proxy   To vote *by proxy*, one member gives written authorization to another member to vote for him. Sometimes a member may vote several proxies; in corporations that allow one vote for each share of stock, a member may be authorized by others to vote hundreds of proxies. Unless specifically provided for in the bylaws of an organization, voting by proxy is not permitted; in the opinion of some, a deliberative assembly would be well advised not to allow it. The procedure conflicts with the basic principle of equality of membership.[1]

Preferential Voting   On a *preferential ballot*, voters mark not only their first choice but also their second, third, and so on, ranking their choices in decreasing order of preference.

Some organizations tend to shy away from any form of preferential voting, as if it involved some sort of trickery. This is unfortunate, because it can save substantial time in the election of officers. A principal advantage of preferential voting is to assure the completion of an election, or of the choice between propositions, with only one ballot. Many organizations could profit by looking into the various forms of preferential and proportional voting and, perhaps, including in their bylaws improved procedures for electing of

[1]Byrl A. Whitney, in "Proxy Voting," *Parliamentary Journal* 6 (January, 1965): 8–12, recommends that parliamentarians urge organizations not to legalize proxy voting by including provisions for it in their bylaws.

officers, members of standing committees, members of boards, and the like.[2]

Voting by preferential ballot is discussed in Chapter 10. When both the "hardware" and the "know-how" are available to an organization, a preferential ballot designed for processing by a computer will greatly simplify the operation.

[2]For further information, see John H. Humphreys, *Proportional Representation* (London: Methuen and Company, Ltd., 1911); E. M. Bacon and Morrill Wyman, *Direct Elections and Law-Making by Popular Vote* (Boston: Houghton Mifflin Company, 1912); W. J. M. MacKenzie, *Free Elections* (New York: Holt Rinehart and Company, 1958); Robert W. English, "A Realistic View of the Hare System of Preferential Balloting," 3rd ed. (Chicago: The American Institute of Parliamentarians, 1964); and *Robert's Rules of Order Newly Revised* (Glenview, Ill.: Scott, Foresman and Company, 1970), pp. 357–360.

Nominations and Elections 10

Nominations
and Elections

Elections held by relatively small informal volunteer organizations need not be complicated. On the day of the announced election, the presiding officer asks for nominations from the floor for the office of, say, president. Perhaps one, two, or three candidates are nominated. When a pause indicates that no further nominations are forthcoming, the presiding officer announces that the nominations are closed, and instructs the tellers to distribute the ballots.

The presiding officer requests every member to indicate his choice by writing a nominee's name on the ballot, folding the ballot, and passing it to the aisle for collection by a teller. When all the ballots have been collected, including those of the presiding officer, the secretary, and the tellers, the ballots are canvassed by the tellers. *Canvassing* the ballots means more than just counting. It includes evaluating ballots to identify those that are invalid, blank, cast for illegal nominees, illegible, abstaining, and the like, and reporting the total results to the presiding officer for his announcement of the results.

If a nominee has received a majority of the votes cast, the presiding officer announces the winner of the election. Nominations are then in order for the next office, and the procedure is repeated until each office has been filled. In the majority of cases, there are no complications.

Since one must be ready, however, to deal with complicated situations that can arise in elections, this chapter will discuss in more detail the selection of nominees and some variations in the voting process. Organizations should include in their bylaws a description of all offices, and the eligibility qualifications, duties, and terms of office for each. The bylaws should also include necessary instructions for conducting the elections of members to office.

Nominations

Theoretically, each member has the right to nominate the candidate of his choice for each office to be filled. But when members view objectively the qualifications and experience required for a particular office, and the likelihood of their nominee being elected, the field of eligible candidates is narrowed considerably. Furthermore, it often happens that an experienced, qualified member cannot, in all fairness, permit his name to be offered in nomination because he has too little time, or poor health, or because his job takes him out of town too often, or for other similar reasons. When all factors have been considered, there is usually rather a narrow field of nominees available.

From the Floor

When nominations are called for from the floor, a member may rise and state, "Mr. Chairperson, I nominate Joe Smith for treasurer." The presiding officer acknowledges the nomination, usually by saying, "Joe Smith has been nominated. Are there other nominations?" Nominations do not need a second, although seconding speeches are sometimes presented in support of a candidate. In small assemblies members often make their nominations while remaining seated. The secretary records the nominations in the minutes. If only one candidate is nominated for an office, the presiding officer may, unless the rules require a vote by ballot, announce, "Since Mr. Smith is the only nominee for the office of treasurer, and a ballot vote is not required, I hereby declare him elected, if there is no objection."

When one or more candidates have been nominated and further nominations appear not to be forthcoming, the presiding officer should declare the nominations closed and proceed with the election. A motion To Close the Nominations (discussed in Chapter 6) is not necessary, and even if passed could not prevent members from writing the names of the candidates of their choice on their ballots, whether or not they had been formally nominated.

If the number of nominees appears to be becoming cumbersome, the presiding officer may explain that too many nominees overly complicates the voting process and remind the members that other offices are also to be filled. Usually such a statement will prompt a few nominees, sensing that they have little chance of being elected, to withdraw their names. Too many nominees is seldom a problem; more frequently the opposite occurs.

With several nominees remaining in the running, the balloting should proceed. If there is a large number of nominees, it may be agreed by a majority vote *before* the balloting that the two or three candidates receiving the least votes on the first ballot will be dropped, and if necessary the process repeated, until one nominee receives a majority vote. The use of preferential balloting, discussed later in this chapter, makes only one ballot necessary in such cases.

By Committee

In larger organizations, many of which meet only at the time of their annual convention, nominations from the floor are not considered practical. A *nominating committee* serves the important function of selecting nominees, and the bylaws of the organization may stipulate that nominations will not be received from the floor. The committee's members may be appointed or elected, according to the bylaws. It is preferable that the committee be elected, since this procedure prevents the president or presiding officer from appointing to the committee only those who will nominate candidates who favor continuing his policies. The committee must be large enough to be representative of various interest groups and geographic areas. Thus a nominating committee with twelve or fifteen members, or more, is not unusual. If provided for in the bylaws, the member receiving the largest number of votes may be declared the presiding officer. If no such provision is made, the members may elect their own presiding officer.

Sometimes a nominating committee, in addition to making nominations for offices, nominates a list of members, perhaps two or three times the size of the committee, for election, usually by mail, to the next nominating committee. This procedure assures continuity. It is often stipulated that a member is not eligible to serve more than two terms in succession, or more than a total of a certain number of years, to prevent the committee from perpetuating itself.

The nominating committee may meet several times to draw up a slate of candidates for its report. Committees whose members are widely scattered geographically may circulate lists of names among the members by mail, or hold telephone conferences, to narrow the number of candidates. Normally, the committee must complete its report in time for inclusion in the program of the annual meeting, or the meeting designated for the election. The committee should, of course, secure a member's agreement to serve if elected, before his name is included in the report of nominees.

Unless prohibited in the bylaws, nominations from the floor are requested by the presiding officer after the nominating committee has made its report, and nominees so selected are added to those nominated by the committee. No action is taken on the report of a nominating committee; the nominations it presents are treated as if they had been made by members from the floor.

The nominating committee may present only one name for an office, or more, depending on instructions in the bylaws and on the committee's preferences. Organizations may require in their bylaws that the committee nominate at least two candidates for each office, but this is not frequently done. Candidates with little chance of election should not be nominated just to insure the voters a choice.

Some organizations provide for nominations by petition. In these cases, the bylaws instruct members that petitions bearing a specified number of signatures sponsoring a candidate will be accepted by a certain date prior to the election; usually the organization supplies the appropriate forms to be used. Petitions judged to be in order result in the candidate's name being placed in nomination as if nominated from the floor. All details governing nomination by petition should be spelled out in the bylaws. A common error in formulating rules providing for nominating by petition is to require too many signatures.

By Petition

Most organizations state in their bylaws that voting in elections will be conducted by secret ballot, or simply by ballot. A vote by ballot is usually taken to mean that voting is conducted so as to prevent disclosure of the members' votes. Voting by ballot should normally be used in all instances in which a member's vote, if disclosed, could be used to his disadvantage.

Elections

The most common ballot is a small piece of blank paper. The presiding officer requests that members vote by writing on the ballot the name of the candidate of their choice for the office in question.

Voting

If the nominees' names are written on a blackboard and clearly numbered, the candidate's number may be used instead of his name. The usual procedure is to take separate votes for each office. Alternatively, a ballot may be printed including the names of all nominees for all offices; and the voter selects his choice for each office by marking an "X" in the appropriate space. A disadvantage of this method over balloting for each office separately is that losing nominees for major offices have no opportunity to be elected to lesser offices; that is, a losing nominee for president has lost his opportunity to be considered for vice president. The printed ballot is frequently used to elect officers of large organizations by mail. Enclosures outlining the qualifications of the candidates may be mailed with the ballots.

The presiding officer should conduct the election, not let it get out of hand. He should follow the procedure closely at each step. He makes sure that each member has a ballot, and instructs the members to "Please mark your ballot" by using an agreed upon procedure, then, after a slight pause, he requests that all ballots be folded and handed to the tellers. Before ballots are collected he assures himself that all members have voted who wish to vote by inquiring, "Has each member present voted who wishes to vote?" If all have voted, he should announce, "The balloting is closed, and the tellers will please collect the ballots." Sometimes a brief recess is declared to await the results of canvassing the ballots.

The Use of Tellers   When voting by ballot has been planned in advance, such as for an election, the presiding officer should be ready to announce his selection of *tellers*, having probably secured their permission beforehand to serve. When a ballot vote has not been anticipated, the presiding officer will appoint tellers as needed. Usually, no less than three tellers are chosen, with the first named as chief teller. The chief teller divides the assembly into sections, and assigns each teller to distribute and collect the ballots in his section. He also sees that the presiding officer and secretary, as well as the tellers themselves, are given ballots.

When all ballots appear to have been collected, the presiding officer inquires, "Have all the ballots been collected?" If so, he directs the tellers to retire to the place selected for canvassing. In votes, including elections, highly charged with emotional tension, the presiding officer may invite one or more members representing opposing points of view to observe the canvassing, with a firm understanding that they are only observers. In extreme cases, ballots may be canvassed in full view of the assembly.

When the ballots have been canvassed, the complete tally may be recorded as follows:

1.	Votes for	36
2.	Votes against	33
3.	Blank ballots	3
4.	Marked but invalid ballots	1
5.	Abstentions	2
6.	Total eligible valid votes cast	69
7.	Number required to pass (win)	36
8.	Result (Motion passed or lost; or ——— elected)	Passed

Marked but invalid (spoiled) ballots include those that cannot be deciphered and those cast for ineligible candidates. Also, two or more ballots folded together are counted as one illegal ballot. Errors in spelling do not make a ballot invalid if the intent of the voter is obvious. Blank ballots and those marked "abstaining" do not count in the total number of ballots cast as a basis for determining what constitutes a majority, although they may provide useful information toward determining the presence of a quorum. Invalid ballots do count in the total vote cast for determining a majority.

The chief teller presents the report to the presiding officer, who, after making sure he understands the report, announces the results. The ballots

Announcing the Results

should be sealed in an envelope and given to the secretary, who keeps them at least until after the next meeting of the organization in case either a question arises requiring a check on the vote count, or the assembly orders a recanvassing of the ballots.

Use of the Preferential Ballot

Some organizations use ballots that permit the voter to indicate not only his first choice but also his second and third choices, and so forth. This method has the major advantage of providing for the election of several nominees by one ballot, making unnecessary repeated balloting. For example, several members may be elected to a board, or faculty members to at-large membership on a college senate, on one ballot. One disadvantage of this method is that it may take longer to count the votes.

The ballot that follows is a sample ballot for preferential voting, adaptable for use by organizations.

If, at the end of the balloting, any nominee has a majority of first-choice votes in the total number of eligible votes cast, he is declared elected. If no nominee has a majority, the preferential ballot makes possible the use of second- and third-choice preferences to determine winning candidates. There are two ways to handle the ballots at this point; most tellers start by arranging the ballots in separate piles, according to first-choice votes for nominees.

Under the English system, sometimes called a Single Transferrable Vote System, the nominee who has the smallest number of first choices is dropped, and each ballot in his pile is "transferred" to that of the nominee ranked second. If the second choice on any ballot is a nominee already declared elected, the third choice on the ballot is "transferred" to the pile of the third-choice nominee. If, as a result of this transfer, any nominee receives a majority, he is declared elected. If there are only three nominees, and a tie results between the remaining two after

Preferential Ballot

Instructions: Vote for not more than 4 nominees. Mark your preferences by using 1, 2, 3, 4, with 1 representing your first choice, etc. Do not give any "tie" rankings.

FOR PRESIDENT

CANDIDATE	RANK
Jonathan Bryan	
Nathan Close	2
Freeman Cousins	4
James Finney	
Elmer Hines	3
Oliver Johnson	
John Lawson	1

dropping the third, the tie is decided in favor of the nominee who has the most original first choices. When there are more than three nominees, and when no winner is determined after the first transfer, the process is repeated. The transferred votes are added to the original totals, and the remaining nominee with the least number of first choice votes is dropped; his ballots are transferred in the manner described above.

The process is repeated until the required number of nominees receive majority votes, or until the number of "ballot piles" is reduced to the number of nominees to be elected. This method gives considerable weight to first-choice selections and, of course, prevents a nominee from winning who might, theoretically, have received all the second-choice votes.

Under what is called the American system, the nominee having the least number of first choices is dropped, but his ballots are not made use of in any way. Instead, the second-choice votes received by the remaining nominees are added to the first choices received by each, and a nominee is declared elected if the total of his first and second choices constitute a majority. If the new total is still short of a majority, the elimination process is repeated. The ballots of the nominee having the least number of combined first and second choices are eliminated, and the third choices received by the remaining nominees are added to the first and second choices each has received; the nominee who now has the highest number of first, second, and third choices is declared elected, assuming he has a majority of the eligible votes cast. A tie between two or more nominees is usually resolved in the same manner as under the English system.

Another plan, sometimes called the West Australian Plan, or the Hare–Ware system, is an outgrowth of the electoral reforms advanced by Sir Thomas Hare in England in 1857. In this system, if only one nominee is to be elected, the first-choice ballots are counted and, if no one receives a majority, all but the two leading nominees are dropped. The ballots cast for defeated nominees are divided between the two remaining nominees in accordance with the preferences indicated on these ballots. Advocates of the West Australian Plan believe it the simplest in operation and the best method to reflect the will of the majority.

Still another method is the "low total" plan. This involves adding the "choices" cast for each nominee—that is, 1 for first choice, 2 for second choice, and so on—and declaring the nominees with the lowest total votes to be the winners. A random number, usually the number following the total number of nominees being elected, should be assigned to all unranked nominees on each ballot to assure that the total number of votes being added in each case is the same.

Voting by preferential ballot is not as desirable as direct voting by secret ballot in an organizational meeting. But when several nominees are to be elected at the same time, the preferential ballot saves valuable time for the assembly by delegating the job of counting to a few tellers. Prior agreement on the method of counting the preferential ballots is essential, since the various methods may not give identical results. And if nominees are to be elected by a plurality vote, authorization must be granted under the bylaws. A request that voters rank only the number of nominees to be elected will help the tellers. Members should be told that to give the same rankings to two or more nominees may invalidate their ballots.

Organizations interested in using preferential ballots should appoint members to study the various methods available and devise a ballot form suitable for their use.

Constitutions, Bylaws, and Rules

11

Constitutions,
Bylaws, and Rules

Organizations traditionally have a constitution and a set of bylaws.[1] Very few have separate rules of order and standing rules. Organizations vary considerably in the degree of formality they use to state their basic rules and objectives. Each organization will need to decide for itself what form best suits its needs. A volunteer organization with a minimum of business to conduct in its meetings may get along well with only an undetailed set of bylaws articulating its name, purpose, committee structure, officers, and the like. A constitution may be eliminated entirely if the bylaws are rewritten to contain the information that formerly appeared in the constitution. For complex organizations, it is probably preferable to state rules of order and standing rules separately, to incorporate other data in a set of bylaws, omitting a constitution. Most groups find bylaws alone satisfactory.

Constitutions and Bylaws

A constitution usually consists of various "articles," designated by Roman numerals, each made up of many "sections" and "paragraphs" covering the subject matter of the article. A constitution always includes a procedure by which the constitution may be amended, stipulating how much advance notice is required of intention

[1]A more complete and technical discussion of this subject may be found in *Sturgis Standard Code of Parliamentary Procedure*, 2nd ed. (New York: McGraw-Hill, 1966), pp. 202–214.

Sample Bylaws, Standing Rules, and Rules of Order

(Name of Organization)

to amend, and how large a vote is required to adopt proposed amendments. Bylaws contain more specific information outlining the implementation of general policies stated in the constitution. Rules of order generally include procedural rules that vary from those stated in the

of preferential balloting if desired.
- C. Votes required to elect
- D. Provision for election without ballot of unopposed nominees
9. Quorum
- A. For assembly meetings
- B. For committees
10. Organizational discipline
- A. Nonpayment or late payment of dues
- B. For Disciplining of members for other reasons
- C. Procedure for bringing charges, conducting hearings, impeaching, or suspending members
- D. Reinstatement procedures
11. Adoption of parliamentary authority
- A. Provision for adopting and for changing selection of parliamentary authority
- B. Application of authority with respect to adopted rules of order
12. Procedure for Amending bylaws

STANDING RULES
1. Time for meetings to begin
2. Location of meetings
3. Policy on guests at meetings
4. Policy on special meetings closed to guests
5. Guest speakers
6. Responsibility for refreshments
7. Responsibility for lighting, noise control, public address system, heating, and the like.
8. Procedure for amending standing rules

RULES OF ORDER
1. The order of business
2. Special rules governing length of speeches
3. Methods of voting, including authorization for mail ballots and preferential ballots
4. Conditions under which a plurality vote is acceptable in place of a majority vote
5. Procedural rules that differ from those in the parliamentary authority
6. Procedure for amending rules of order

adopted parliamentary authority. Standing rules deal with relatively minor points of organizational operation and require only a majority vote to change, while amendment of the bylaws and rules of order often requires previous notice of intent and a two-thirds vote.

Whether or not an organization has all four types of rules—a constitution, bylaws, rules of order, and standing rules—the essential information includes the official name and purpose of the organization, and details regarding membership, officers and their duties, terms of office, election procedures, standing committees, provisions for meetings, the quorum, the adopted parliamentary authority, and requirements for adoption of amendments.

Many organizations would profit from a thorough study and revision of their constitutions and bylaws. Such a study might well result in a clearer and more up-to-date instrument, all of whose provisions are incorporated in a set of bylaws. Since constitutions and bylaws are adequately treated elsewhere,[2] this discussion will be limited to some general topics.

The adoption of an original constitution and/or set of bylaws requires only a majority vote. After adoption, the rules for amending will be those stated in the constitution and bylaws. The recommendation of a committee on bylaws (the term "bylaws" will be used to refer to both constitution and bylaws) is considered in the same way as is any motion embodying a committee recommendation, and is subject to the same amendments, referrals, and postponements as any other main motion. The appropriate motion from the committee is not, "I move the adoption of the committee report," but "I move that the following bylaws be adopted . . ."

Amendments to bylaws may be proposed by any member in good standing. Unless a procedure is developed to handle such requests, however, difficult situations may arise in meetings in which several individuals propose to amend the bylaws immediately, *if possible under the bylaws,* or announce their intention to propose amendments

---

[2]Model constitutions, bylaws, and rules are available in the books listed in the bibliography by Davidson, Demeter, O'Brien, and Sturgis. Davidson includes, in addition, a checklist of eighteen "booby traps" (pp. 200–202) against which a new constitution or set of bylaws may be checked for errors or omissions.

Modern Parliamentary Procedure

at the next meeting, if notice of intent is required at a prior meeting. Proposed amendments must be carefully considered to insure that they are consistent with existing policy as stated in the bylaws. Also, the language of a proposed amendment ought to be in keeping with that generally used in the bylaws.

A procedure adopted by some organizations to handle this situation appears to work well. A standing committee, possibly one on bylaw revision or on organization and rules, is charged with accepting proposed amendments, evaluating their merits, rewording them when necessary, and proposing them as main motions with committee recommendations for action by the assembly. This procedure is not meant to prevent members from proposing amendments, but to give their proposals a better chance for favorable consideration and adoption.

Sometimes organizations make it very difficult to amend their bylaws by requiring too large a number of members to vote for the change in order to pass it. This seems to arise from reluctance to change bylaws that have been labored over and extensively discussed in meetings and hearings. But often the changes are needed only a brief time after adopting the bylaws. It is a question of what constitutes responsible action by an assembly; leeway for correction of error should be ample.

Therefore, most organizations should probably permit amendment of the bylaws by no more than a two-thirds vote, or a majority vote provided previous notice has been given. The requirements of some organizations that the bylaws be amended by a two-thirds vote of the membership following previous notice, or a two-thirds vote of members present following previous notice, are difficult to fulfill—perhaps too difficult.

Organizations should include in their bylaws authorization for the presiding officer to declare an unopposed nominee elected without a ballot, if no one objects. This eliminates the awkward and undemocratic alternative of the secretary casting a ballot for the assembly declaring a nominee, if unopposed, elected. If a single member objects, of course, a ballot should be required; members should be privileged to submit blank ballots, or ballots bearing the name of any eligible candidate as well as that of the single announced nominee. The recommended procedure is not a unanimous vote but a vote without objection—if such is the case.

Most authorities agree that bylaws may not be suspended. But confusion sometimes arises when an organization wishes temporarily to suspend a rule of order or a standing rule, and the rule in question is found to be included in the bylaws. The problem here is not the one of legality, but of recognition that the rule should have been separately listed under an appropriate heading. The principle that bylaws may not be suspended is sound. However, a rule of order that has been incorporated into a bylaw may be suspended.

Standing Rules Standing rules cover nonprocedural subjects. They may not be stated in the adopted parliamentary authority, but are considered desirable to operate effectively. They are usually of minor importance by comparison with rules of order, and may therefore be authorized, deleted, or suspended by majority vote, unless an organization wishes to require otherwise. Some examples of standing rules are:

1. All scheduled meetings shall begin promptly at eight o'clock P.M.
2. Unless members are notified to the contrary, all meetings will be held in Brown Auditorium.
3. Guest speakers may receive honoraria of more than one hundred dollars only if approved in advance by the executive committee.
4. Any member who misses three meetings in succession, without providing a suitable excuse to the secretary, is subject to a fine not to exceed ten dollars.
5. Members may bring guests to all meetings except those described in the bylaws as closed meetings.

Rules of order are those rules that govern the con- **Rules of Order**
duct of business by an organization: its par-
liamentary procedure. The parliamentary authority adopted as a procedural guide should be
stipulated in the bylaws, since it should not be
possible to suspend the parliamentary authority
by suspending the rules, but only by amending
the bylaw adopting it.

Any rule of order may be suspended (see To
Suspend the Rules in Chapter 5), including rules
stated in the adopted parliamentary authority, as
long as they are limited to procedural rules controlling the conduct of business. However, the
following rules, which are not rules of order, may
not be suspended:

1. Conditions that govern the notice required to
   call a meeting
2. Quorum specifications
3. Specific voting methods, such as a requirement of secret ballots in elections
4. The vote required for particular purposes or
   motions
5. Provisions that protect absentee members
6. Provisions that prevent suspending a bylaw
7. Any provision that, if suspended, would deprive members of their basic rights.

Under rules of order should be listed all those
special procedural rules adopted by an organization that differ from those stated in the adopted
parliamentary authority; these rules, which, of
course, take priority over those in the adopted
authority, may include the following:

1. The adopted order of business
2. Special rules governing the length of speeches
3. Methods of voting
4. Votes required to elect officers and committee
   members, if different from those specified in
   the adopted parliamentary authority.

Normally, a two-thirds vote is required to
suspend temporarily a rule of order, or to amend
it, unless an assembly wishes to provide in its
bylaws that a majority vote is sufficient following prior notice of intent to amend.

Annotated Bibliography

Annotated Bibliography

Auer, J. Jeffery. *Essentials of Parliamentary Proce-* **Books**
dure. 3rd ed. New York: Appleton-
Century-Crofts, 1959. 57 pp. A brief, clear restatement of *Robert's Rules*. Organizes motions by purpose: To Suppress Debate, To Delay
Action, To Prevent Action, and the like.

Cushing, Luther S. *Manual of Parliamentary Practice*: Rules for Proceeding and Debate in
Deliberative Assemblies. Revised and amplified
by Paul E. Lowe. Philadelphia: David McKay
Company, 1925. 318 pp. See remarks on pages
23–24 in this book.

Davidson, Henry A. *Handbook of Parliamentary
Procedure*. New York: Ronald Press, 1968. 300
pp. Largely a restatement of *Robert's Rules*,
except for the abandonment of The Previous
Question. Includes interesting chapters on
"How Not to Get Pushed Around," "How to
Handle a Heckler," and "Warehouse of Forms
and Documents."

Demeter, George. *Demeter's Manual of Parliamentary Law and Procedure*, blue book edition. Boston: Little, Brown, and Company, 1969. 374 pp.
A "revised, expanded, and updated" version of
the book by the same title privately published
in 1948 and revised several times before the 1969
edition. A restatement of *Robert's Rules*, it is
very detailed and perhaps overly organized and

lengthy. Includes many examples from the author's experiences in parliamentary practice. In Chapter 15, decisions from "500 court cases" are woven into statements of principles that will "help minimize, or avoid altogether, costly law suits."

English, Robert W. *A Realistic View of the Hare System of Preferential Balloting.* 3rd ed. Chicago: The American Institute of Parliamentarians, 1964. 24 pp. Available from 3½ West Main Street, American Institute of Parliamentarians, Room 211–213, Marshalltown, Iowa 50158. Advantages and disadvantages of the Hare System, illustrations of its use, and detailed rules for canvassing ballots marked under the Hare system. Sample ballots included.

Hellman, Hugo. *Parliamentary Procedure.* New York: Macmillan Company, 1966. 113 pp. This textbook presents twenty-seven "lessons" organized around three major divisions: Participating as a Member, Presiding as Chairman, and Broadening Your Knowledge. Its "functional and practical approach" provides class exercises for practice and illustrative dialogues. An admirable attempt to simplify *Robert's Rules* is found in his discussion of "The Core Procedure" and "Special Emergency Procedures," and in his liberalization of the traditional precedence of motions.

Jefferson, Thomas. *A Manual of Parliamentary Practice.* New York: Clark and Maynard, 1867. 196 pp. See remarks on page 22–23 in this book.

Mason, Paul. *Mason's Manual of Legislative Procedure for Legislative and Other Governmental Bodies.* New York: McGraw-Hill Book Company, 1953. 640 pp. Written especially to meet the needs of "legislative and administrative bodies." The rules discussed are taken from judicial decisions and legislative precedents. Not intended as a parliamentary guide for voluntary organizations. Footnotes carry references to the many court decisions cited in the text.

O'Brien, Joseph F. *Parliamentary Law for the Layman*. New York: Harper and Brothers, 1952. 248 pp. A down-to-earth, common-sense approach, pleading for no more formal use of *Robert's Rules* than necessary. Advocates adapting formality of procedure to the degree of unity or division within a group on the question under consideration, and to the size of the group and its knowledge of parliamentary procedure. Written in a clear informal style.

Robert, Henry M. *Robert's Rules of Order Newly Revised*. Glenview, Ill.: Scott, Foresman and Company, 1970. 594 pp. The latest edition of this widely adopted parliamentary authority. See remarks on page 24 in this book.

Sturgis, Alice. *Sturgis Standard Code of Parliamentary Procedure*, 2nd ed. New York: McGraw-Hill Book Company, 1966. 283 pp. One of the best and most comprehensive works. Clarifies and adds to *Robert's Rules*, and differs from it in minor ways, such as substituting "Vote Immediately" and "Postpone Temporarily" for the confusing "Previous Question" and "Lay on the Table" motions. The second edition continues to emphasize conformity of procedure with court decisions, and adds special chapters on parliamentary procedure for labor organizations, conventions, finances, staff and consultants.

Periodicals

The following periodicals print many articles of interest to the student of parliamentary procedure, some of which are listed below.

Adult Leadership. Published monthly, except for July and August, by the Adult Education Association of the United States of America. May, 1952–. Malcolm S. Knowles. "Move Over Mr. Robert" 1 (June, 1952): 2–4. A special issue on "Rules of Freedom and Order," 5 (December, 1956) includes the following articles of interest: Joseph F. O'Brien. "The Use and Abuse of Parliamentary Procedure." 178–182.

William S. Tacy. "The Chair Recognizes—" 183–184. J. Jeffery Auer. "The Role of Chairman—in Committee and Assembly." 188–190. Alice Sturgis. "Putting Parliamentary Procedure to work." 190–192.

Parliamentary Journal. Published in January, April, July, and October by The American Institute of Parliamentarians. March, 1960–. Regularly includes articles of interest, including reviews, reports of research, and informal expressions of opinions by scholars and authorities on parliamentary procedure.

The Quarterly Journal of Speech. Published in February, April, October, and December by the Speech Communication Association. 1915–. (Under present title since February, 1928; from 1915 to 1918, *The Quarterly Journal of Public Speaking*; from 1918 to 1929. *The Quarterly Journal of Speech Education*.) G. W. Gray. "A Philosophy of Parliamentary Law" 27 (October, 1941): 437–441.

J. F. O'Brien. "Henry M. Robert as Presiding Officer" 42 (April, 1956): 157–162.

Speech Monographs. Published in March, June, August, and November by the Speech Communication Association, formerly Speech Association of America. September 1934–.
Kirt E. Montgomery. "Thomas B. Reed's Theory and practice of Congressional Debating" 17 (March, 1950): 65–74.
G. W. Gray. "Thomas Jefferson's Interest in Parliamentary Practice" 27 (November, 1960): 315–322.

Today's Speech. Published in February, April, September, and November by The Eastern Communication Association. 1953–.
Ray E. Keesey. "Don't Ask the Parliamentarian" 8 (November, 1960): 15.
Milton J. Wiksell. "Teaching Parliamentary Procedure to Adults" 9 (February, 1961): 15–16.
J. Calvin Callaghan. "Do Ask the Parliamentarian—Beforehand" 9 (February, 1961): 21.

A special issue, 4 (November, 1956), on "Parliamentary Procedure" includes the following articles:

Alice Sturgis. "American Voluntary Associations: Our Informal Government." 7–9.

Paul Mason. "The Legal Side of Parliamentary Procedure." 9–14.

J. Walter Reeves. "Nominations and Elections in Voluntary Organizations." 15–16.

J. F. O'Brien. "The Chairman and His Job." 19–20.

Exercises

Exercises

1. What is your understanding of decision making "by consensus"?

2. Who decides when consensus has been arrived at in a meeting?

3. Present a five-minute oral report on the Quaker method of decision making.

4. Is it possible for a group to arrive at a decision without using parliamentary procedure? Without applying any of the basic principles of parliamentary procedure?

5. What are the four basic principles of parliamentary procedure?

6. What guidelines serve to determine the appropriate degree of formality in a group meeting?

7. Is there a conflict between the principle that majority rule may not be suspended and the requirement of a two-thirds vote to limit debate? Explain.

8. How can you explain the statement that a "legal majority vote may in fact be a majority of a minority"?

9. Differentiate between the protection of minority rights in parliamentary situations and the struggle by minority groups to attain their constitutional rights.

10. It has been stated that when groups are capable of decision making without formal procedural rules they need not observe any rules. How should the word "capable" be interpreted in this regard?

11. Read Chapter IV, "Jon Stone and the Fools Across the Table," pp. 43–59, in Irving J. Lee's *How To Talk With People* (New York: Harper & Row, 1952), and give a brief report to the class on the problem it discusses.

Chapter 3
Introduction to the
Rules of Procedure

1. Define *precedence of motions*.

2. What flexibility is provided to vary from the established rules governing precedence of motions?

3. Can you think of any circumstances when the seconding of a motion should be required?

4. Explain the "disappearing quorum" and some of its implications for voting.

5. If a quorum is present, could democratic decisions still be made with only ten percent of a quorum voting? Explain.

6. What actions may be taken by a group in the absence of a quorum?

7. In the absence of a quorum for a required meeting, must the meeting be rescheduled? Explain your answer.

8. If you were presiding officer, how would you reply to members insisting "that we go ahead with the meeting anyway," with one member short of a quorum?

9. What is an example of an emergency situation requiring action by a group that would justify taking such action in the absence of a quorum?

10. If the presiding officer rules that normal business may not be conducted since the

meeting is one member short of a quorum, and an appeal to this ruling is upheld by a majority vote, is the principle of majority rule violated if the group does not proceed with its meeting as if a quorum were present?

1. Prepare a resolution with three or four "whereas" clauses preceding the "resolved, that" clause. Notice how closely the parts must relate to each other logically if the resolution is to make sense.

2. Why may main motions stated in a negative form result in confusion in voting?

3. What is meant by the terms *qualified* and *unqualified* in relation to a motion?

4. How many times may a main motion be amended? A motion To Refer to a committee? A motion To Postpone?

5. Which motions discussed in this chapter may be used strategically by an opponent of a motion to delay action on it? By an advocate to expedite action on it?

6. *Using the style of direct address*, state exactly what the presiding officer should say in each of the following instances:
   a. A main motion, a proposed amendment, and a motion To Refer to a committee are all pending. The motion To Postpone consideration until the next meeting is voted on and carried.
   b. On a motion To Limit Debate on a proposed amendment, the vote is 9 for and 5 against.
   c. With a main motion pending, the motion To Recess until the following day is made, followed immediately by the motion To Adjourn.

7. Prepare three exercises like the three above, for class drill.

8. If a motion, such as a proposed amendment to the bylaws, requires a two-thirds vote to pass, how can one defend allowing a proposed amendment to the motion to pass with a majority vote?

9. Under what circumstance are proposed amendments to a motion, although in order, not debatable?

10. Is the motion To Close Debate in order when applied to an undebatable motion? Answer after reading *Robert's Rules of Order Newly Revised* (1970), pp. 162, 168, and 198.

Chapter 5
Special Motions

1. In voting on an appeal, why shouldn't the presiding officer put the question as, "Those in favor of the appeal" and "those against"?

2. What would be an example of the motion To Appeal treated as a main motion?

3. To Withdraw may be either a request, not requiring a vote, or a motion, requiring a vote. Explain.

4. Why should it not be possible to reconsider the vote on the motion To Reconsider? On the motion To Rescind?

5. *Using the style of direct address,* state exactly what the presiding officer should say in each of the following instances:
   a. A main motion is under consideration, and a member other than the mover of the motion moves that it be withdrawn.
   b. A main motion is under consideration, and the presiding officer rules that a proposed amendment is not germane. The ruling is appealed. Follow through the appeal, assuming the vote upholds the appeal.
   c. With a main motion and a proposed amendment pending, a member moves To Suspend the Rules and close debate on both the proposed amendment and the main motion.

Modern Parliamentary Procedure

d. In (c) above, assume that debate is ordered closed and the vote on the proposed amendment is carried.

e. Prepare three exercises like the four above, drawing from both ordinary and special motions, for class drill.

6. Why isn't a Point of Order debatable? How can one defend its being in order "at any time"? And if it "is not a motion at all," what is it?

7. Explain what is meant by the statement that "there is no appeal from a decision by the assembly."

8. Since the motion To Reconsider is debatable, and permits debate on the motion under reconsideration, what is to prevent a member from moving To Reconsider just to gain the opportunity to discuss the motion further even though he expects to vote against the motion To Reconsider?

9. Would it be in order to move To Rescind the action taken at a previous meeting To Reconsider the vote on a motion passed in that meeting? Explain your answer fully.

10. May the mover of a motion prevent a vote To Withdraw his motion by objecting to its withdrawal?

11. Not all experts agree that any member should be eligible to move To Reconsider the vote on a motion. Read what Cushing, Robert, and Sturgis (see footnote 1 in Chapter 5) say on this point, and present your point of view in class.

1. Do you usually think you know how the presiding officer stands on motions discussed in organizations in which you participate? How does the presiding officer reveal his partiality?

**Chapter 7
Conducting the
Meeting**

2. Which term do you prefer: chairman, chairwoman, chairperson? Why?

3. What are some signs that the presiding officer has lost control of his role as leader?

4. Enlarge upon the statement that "the way the presiding officer interprets his role will determine the 'climate' of the group's deliberations."

5. Are you persuaded that a chairman by decree may not be viewed as an impartial presiding officer?

6. Is it a prerequisite of a "parliamentary meeting" that the presiding officer be elected by the members?

7. Have you ever participated in a parliamentary meeting in which some members dominated the proceedings? If so, what did you do about it? What could you have done about it?

8. Report on the most recent meeting you attended, analyzing it in the light of the topics discussed in this chapter.

9. Attend a local town council or state legislature meeting, or any regularly scheduled group meeting in which legislative action is voted, and report on the procedure.

10. Prepare a five-minute oral report on Joseph F. O'Brien's "Henry M. Robert as Presiding Officer," *Quarterly Journal of Speech* 42 (April, 1956): 157–162.

11. Prepare at least two comments a presiding officer might make to prevent a member who has already spoken too much from continuing his remarks. The objective is to be fair but firm, and to make time available to all members who wish to be heard.

**Chapter 8
Committees**

1. Bring to class a committee report from a university or college faculty committee, a local school board, PTA, or civic organization, and analyze it for the class in light of recommendations in this chapter.

2. Explain the reasoning behind the statement that "adoption of a committee's recommendation is entirely different from the authorization of an action proposed in the form of a main motion."

3. Some committee reports are "filed" and some "adopted", but all committee reports must be filed. Explain.

4. A committee recommends in its report that the main motion referred to it be withdrawn, and the committee report is adopted by the assembly. What does the presiding officer say in advising the assembly on the status of the motion referred?

5. Which of the following is preferable for the presiding officer to say at the conclusion of discussion on a committee report: "The report will be filed," "The report has been received," or "The report has been accepted"? Explain why each form is or is not acceptable.

6. Which has more authority, standing committees or special committees? Explain.

7. Most committees consist of an uneven number of members. Why? Is this still a good practice?

8. Why is it a bad practice to elect an *ex officio* member as the presiding officer of a committee?

9. In a committee of seven, what is the minimal number who must approve the committee report before it may be submitted?

10. Enlarge upon the following statement for clarity: "The assembly may not make the committee say something that it did not say."

1. With 79 of a total of 100 members present in a meeting, a majority vote of 5 for and 3 against a motion is declared a valid vote, and

Chapter 9
Voting

the motion carries. How do you defend this situation?

2. What conditions must be fulfilled for a presiding officer validly to declare, "The motion passed unanimously"?

3. A vote on a motion is a tie, 10 for and 10 against. The presiding officer has yet to vote, but there is no point in his voting except for the affirmative. Explain.

4. Explain why an exception is made in the case of an appeal to the rule that a tie vote counts as a negative vote.

5. May a majority vote and a plurality vote, under certain circumstances, be identical? Explain.

6. What are some legitimate reasons a member might abstain from voting? What are some reasons that may not be considered sufficient to record abstaining votes?

7. What is the difference between not voting at all and abstaining from voting?

8. Is returning an unmarked ballot the same as writing "abstaining" on the ballot?

9. May the results of a vote by general consent accurately be announced as a unanimous vote?

10. What are the principal advantages of a show of hands over a voice vote?

11. Under what circumstances may voting by proxy be considered fair? When is it unfair?

Chapter 10
Nominations
and Elections

1. In a recent election a nominee for office ran unopposed but was defeated. How could this happen?

2. Devise a preferential ballot; use it in class to elect a nominating committee; and, following the report of this committee, conduct an

Modern Parliamentary Procedure

election for president, vice president, and secretary–treasurer of the class.

3. What is the difference between a "candidate" and a "nominee." Which comes first?

4. When there is only one nominee in an election, why should not the secretary "cast a unanimous ballot" and declare him elected?

5. Why is the Electoral College system employed in national elections in the United States thought by some to be unfair?

6. A member is elected vice president while he is absent. At the next meeting, he rises to decline the office, stating that he does not want the honor and that he had not been consulted about entering his name as a nominee. If you were presiding, what would you say?

7. As presiding officer, what would you say to a member who insisted on nominating two members for the same office?

8. If each member has the right to nominate the candidate of his choice for office, how can a motion to close nominations be in order without depriving members of their right to nominate? Explain.

9. Under what circumstances are nominations from the floor impractical? Under what circumstances are they prohibited?

10. What are some advantages of a nominating committee elected by the assembly over one appointed by the presiding officer?

11. What action is taken on the report of a nominating committee? If you were presiding officer, and the committee had just finished presenting its report, what would you say?

12. If you were using a preferential ballot in your organization to elect a committee, which

method of counting ballots would you prefer? Why?

1. Request a copy of the constitution, bylaws, and rules of a local organization, and write an evaluation of them.

2. Divide the class into committees of 3, 4, or 5 members. Each group will volunteer its services to a local organization—a student or faculty group, civic organization, labor union, etc.—to study its constitution, bylaws, and rules and recommend changes for clarity and effectiveness. Present the results of all deliberations to your instructor in a conference outside of class time.

3. It is usually more difficult to find a specific item in a constitution than in a simple numbered set of bylaws. Why?

4. How do rules of order differ from standing rules?

5. List at least three different methods used by organizations to propose amendments to their bylaws. Defend the method of your choice.

6. There are several variations in the vote required by organizations to approve proposed amendments to bylaws. List three, and defend your preference.

7. When an organization wishes to suspend a rule of order and finds that it is a part of a bylaw, may it still be suspended? How could this situation be remedied in the future?

8. Should the adoption of a parliamentary authority by an organization be included in the bylaws? The rules of order? The standing rules? What difference does it make?

9. If provisions governing a quorum were placed in the bylaws instead of the rules of order, would this prevent their suspension if the organization were strongly in favor of doing so?

10. Report to the class on the eighteen "booby traps" an organization might encounter while making up a constitution and bylaws, discussed by Henry A. Davidson in *Handbook of Parliamentary Procedure* (New York: Ronald Press, 1968).

Index